Kids' Cooking
step-by-step

THE AUSTRALIAN
Women's Weekly

contents

We've collected great recipes that you'll love cooking for your family and friends. But before you begin, read our tips on the following pages called *Get ready, Get set,* and *Go!*

Select the dish you would like to cook.

A photograph showing you exactly what the finished dish should look like.

Make sure you have all the ingredients before you start to cook.

fabulous fettuccine

This dish will be popular with all the family. There is not too much work to do beforehand and you can use any kind of dried pasta—just check the packet to see how long you should cook it.

ingredients

1 large onion
2 cloves garlic
250g button mushrooms
4 bacon rashers
375g dried fettuccine
2 tablespoons olive oil
300ml cream

★ Serves 4 to 6

1 Cut the onion in half then slice it, crush the garlic and slice the mushrooms. Put the bacon on a chopping board. **Using kitchen scissors, cut the rind from the bacon** then cut the bacon into thin pieces.

2 Put a large saucepan on the stove. Use a jug to pour in enough water to come 1/4 of the way up the side of the pan. Turn the heat to high, cover the pan with a lid and bring the water to the boil. **Using oven mitts, remove the lid and add the fettuccine to the boiling water.** When the water boils again, stir the fettuccine with a wooden spoon.

3 While the fettuccine is cooking, put a large frying pan on the stove, turn the heat to medium and put the oil in the pan. Add the onion, garlic and bacon, and stir until the onion is soft. **Add the mushrooms** and stir until they are soft.

4 **Add the cream to the mushroom mixture** and cook for 5 minutes.

5 **Test the fettuccine by taking a couple of strands from the pan with some tongs**, letting it cool slightly then tasting it. If it is just soft, it is ready. Stand a large strainer in the sink. Using oven mitts take the pan of fettuccine to the sink and pour it into the strainer. Let the water drain away.
Serve the bacon and mushroom sauce over the fettuccine.

Creamy bacon and mushroom fettuccine

Step-by-step pictures make the recipes really easy to follow.

We give you handy hints to make sure every recipe is a success.

Each instruction is numbered to match a picture.

Each picture is explained in words that appear bigger and darker than the others in the step.

get ready

Before you start

Go through the recipes and decide what it is you wish to cook. Check the cupboard, pantry, refrigerator and freezer to make sure you have all the tools and ingredients you need to make the recipe.

Pastry brushes are used to brush butter or oil over pans, etc (this is called greasing). They can also be used to brush water, milk or egg over the-top of foods before they are cooked.

Wire whisks are great for gently mixing 1 ingredient into another or for making lumpy mixtures smooth.

Wooden spoons and spatulas are a safe alternative to metal spoons in the kitchen.

Knives are dangerous! Be careful when using knives of any kind. They come in all shapes and sizes, so choose the right knife for the right purpose — don't use a really large carving knife to peel potatoes! Serrated knives (near right) are great for cutting cakes, slices and tomatoes.

Spatulas can be plastic, rubber, wood or metal (the metal ones are also called egg slides). They are a flat utensil used for scraping out bowls, and lifting or turning foods.

Strainers can be used to sift dry ingredients as well as to drain pasta and vegetables.

A garlic crusher is a handy gadget that makes it easy to crush garlic. If you don't have one, try grating the garlic instead but watch your fingers.

1 cup
(250ml)

Read the recipe

Before you start cooking, check your chosen recipe from beginning to end and make sure you understand each step. If you have any questions, ask an adult in your household for an explanation.

1 tablespoon
(20ml)

Measuring spoons come as a set of 1 tablespoon, 1 teaspoon, 1/2 teaspoon and 1/4 teaspoon. Level the required spoonful with the back of a flat-bladed knife when measuring solid things like spices and sugar. You can measure both liquid or dry ingredients with these spoons.

1 teaspoon
(5ml)

1/2 cup
(125ml)

1/2 teaspoon
(2.5ml)

1/4 teaspoon
(1.25ml)

1/3 cup
(80ml)

Liquid measuring jugs
will have millilitres and cup measurements written down the sides. Place the jug on a level surface and pour the liquid into the jug until it reaches the required amount.

1/4 cup
(60ml)

Measuring cups come in a set of 1 cup, 1/2 cup, 1/3 cup and 1/4 cup. Spoon the ingredient into the required cup size. Drag the back of a flat-bladed knife across the surface to level the top of the ingredient. Sometimes the recipe may direct you to pack the ingredient firmly into the cup.

Kitchen scales are often used to measure food by weight instead of measuring it in spoons or cups.

get set

Dress for success

Cooking is much more fun if you're dressed comfortably, and wearing a clean apron helps save your clothes from getting too dirty. If you have long hair, tie it back or wear a headband, scarf or cap. And don't forget your feet—wear shoes that are closed-in and have non-slip soles—sneakers are perfect.

Get clean

Because you're planning to handle food, it is important to wash your hands well—and often—with soap and warm water. Don't forget to dry them well with a clean towel. It is also a good idea to keep another cloth handy to wipe up any spills. Rinse it out in warm water every time you use it, and remember never to use the same cloth on the floor that you use for the benchtop or for your hands.

Safety first

• NEVER start cooking without first asking an adult if it's okay.

• ALWAYS use oven mitts when putting things into, or taking them out of, a hot oven or the microwave—tea towels are too thin to protect your hands and, since a tea towel is often damp, it will steam when it comes into contact with the heat of the oven or hot pan and could burn your fingers.

• ALWAYS place a heatproof mat or wooden board on the benchtop near the stove so you have somewhere to sit the hot pan when you take it out of the oven or off the stove-top.

• TAKE CARE when using knives or sharp utensils—keep your fingers away from the blades and tips. If

you are not allowed to use sharp knives, ask an adult to help you.

• ALWAYS cut food on a chopping board, not the benchtop.

• NEVER use an electrical appliance near water and never handle any plug when your hands are wet. AND always remember to unplug electrical appliances, such as the toaster or sandwich-maker, before you get close to them with any kind of metal kitchen utensil.

• REMEMBER that pans on the stove-top have steam coming from them, so do not reach across them with an unprotected arm.

• WHEN you put a pan on the stove-top, make sure its handle is not sticking out where it can easily be

knocked over. Turn the pan so the handle is out of your way—but so it's not over the heat either.

• AFTER chopping raw meat, chicken or fish, the chopping board **must** be washed well with soap and hot water before you use it again.

Timely tip

• WHEN a recipe gives a cooking time, set a timer or minute minder for that time—if you don't, it's easy to forget how long your food has been cooking and you could overcook or burn it. AND you should know that if a pan is left bubbling away, without a lid, on the stove for too long, it can boil dry and even burn on the bottom.

• BEFORE you turn on the oven, make sure the shelves are in the right position for whatever you are going to make. For instance, if you are baking a cake, the shelves should be in the middle of the oven. But make sure you leave enough room between the highest shelf and the inside top of the oven for your baking dish or oven tray—and whatever is in or on it! Turn the oven on and wait until it has reached the correct temperature before you put the food in to cook. (Most ovens have a light near the controls which goes out when the set temperature is reached—ask an adult if you are uncertain.)

Setting it straight

• IF you decide to surprise mum or your friends and cook dinner, don't forget that part of the job includes setting the table.

• TRY folding the serviettes into pretty or fun shapes. Or you can use a napkin ring for a special touch.

• IF you use placemats instead of a tablecloth, you're still protecting the table from spills but saving on the washing and ironing.

• THE easiest way to remember the right way to set the cutlery is to put knives and spoons on the right, and forks on the left, with the ones you use first being on the outside of the place setting. Make sure that your dinner guest has enough knives, forks and spoons to use a clean one for each course.

Tidying up

Every family has different ideas about what are good and bad manners at the table. But there is one rule in the kitchen that everyone agrees on—and it's that cleaning-up is a part of cooking. The least favourite part, sure, but do it well and you stand a better chance of being allowed back into the kitchen again for more of the fun part—cooking! If you do just these few things before you eat, then the person who has to do the washing up won't have such a messy kitchen to face after the meal (remember, this could be YOU!):

• FIRST, check that the stove has been turned off (and, when it's cold, wiped free of any spills).

• PUT away all the food you have finished with, checking that lids are on tightly and that raw or fresh foods you haven't used are covered and put in the refrigerator.

• WASH all the dirty utensils in hot soapy water, taking extra care when it comes to knives and other sharp things like food processor blades. Dry everything with a clean cloth and put it back in its right place.

• WIPE the benchtop clean with a hot soapy cloth, sweep the floor and double-check that all electrical appliances have been turned off.

go
the things you need to know

Chopping

Slicing

Making a garnish

• Use a vegetable peeler to make thin ribbons of vegetables like cucumbers or carrots. These ribbons look great in salads or for decorating a plate of cutlets and wedges.

• Remove the rind (the coloured skin—not the white part) from oranges, lemons and limes with a vegetable peeler. Next, cut these slices of rind into really thin strips and sprinkle them over desserts like a fruit salad or orange cake.

• Strawberries are everyone's favourite—cut them into fan-shapes to decorate an ice-cream sundae.

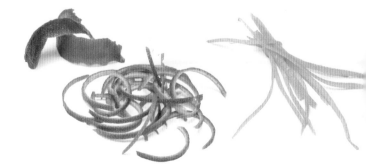

Separating an egg

1 Crack the egg by tapping it with the back of a knife.

2 Break the egg gently in half onto a saucer.

3 Cover the yolk with a glass then tilt the saucer carefully so that the egg white runs into a separate bowl.

1

2

3

Grating

Removing the seed from an avocado

Cut the avocado in half, around the hard seed. Twist the halves in different directions to separate them. Use a spoon to scoop out the seed—then throw the seed away.

Simmering

Simmering means that the liquid you are cooking is bubbling gently.

When you have water, oil or any liquid in a pan that is being heated on top of the stove, always wear oven mitts when touching the pan so that, if you spill any liquid, you won't burn your hands.

Boiling

Boiling means that the bubbles of a liquid are rising rapidly to the top.

Put a tight-fitting lid on a pan of water to make it come to the boil faster.

Shallow-frying means that you are frying something without too much oil in the pan—about 0.5cm of oil will be deep enough.

Always turn the heat to medium and check that the oil is the right temperature before you add the food. A 1cm cube of bread turns golden in colour in about 30 seconds if the oil is hot enough.

Melting chocolate

Melting chocolate in the microwave is really easy and, once you get the hang of it, you will always melt chocolate this way. Break the chocolate into pieces over a microwave-safe bowl. Put the bowl, uncovered, into the microwave oven and cook on HIGH (100%) for

1 minute for every 200g of chocolate. Using oven mitts, take the bowl out of the microwave oven and stir the chocolate. If it hasn't melted, repeat the cooking for another 30 seconds. The chocolate might not look melted— but when it is stirred you will find it is very soft.

Shallow-frying

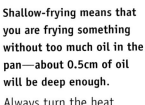

Testing and turning out a cake

1 Using oven mitts, take the cake pan out of the oven. Sit the pan on a wooden board and put a metal skewer into the centre of the cake. Pull the skewer out, and if no cake mixture sticks to it, the cake is cooked.

2 Turn the cake upside down onto a wire cake rack then remove the pan and the lining paper.

3 Put another rack over the cake and, holding the two racks like a sandwich, turn the cake over.

Lining and greasing a cake pan

1 Trace a circle around the base of the pan onto a piece of greaseproof or baking paper. Cut out the circle, on the inside of the mark, with a pair of scissors.

2 Brush inside the pan with vegetable oil or melted butter.

3 Put the paper circle over the base of the pan, press it down and smooth out any little wrinkles.

Filling and using a piping bag

Place the nozzle you wish to use into the narrow end of the piping bag. Stand the bag in a glass, nozzle-side down, and turn the top of the bag over the glass so you can easily spoon the piping mixture into it.

Now remove the bag from the glass and twist the top of the bag to stop the mixture squishing out the top.

Practise piping different shapes, such as stars, swirls or wiggly lines, on a plate before you set to work on your masterpiece.

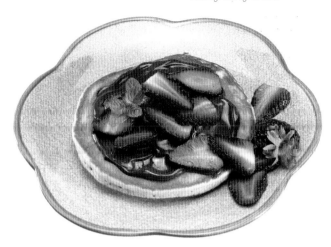

Nutty berry treat

Lemon, butter and sugar

hassle-free hotcakes

You will need to start making the hotcakes about 1 hour before you're ready to eat them. The batter has to stay in the refrigerator for $1/2$ hour before the cooking starts.

Bananas with maple syrup

ingredients

1³/₄ cups self-raising flour

¹/₄ teaspoon bicarbonate of soda

2 eggs

1¹/₄ cups milk

¹/₃ cup caster sugar

30g soft butter

★ *Makes 10*

1 **Sift the flour and bicarbonate of soda** into a large bowl.

2 **Make a hole in the centre of the flour** with your fingers.

3 Break the eggs into a large jug. Add the milk and sugar and **beat with a fork until mixed together.**

4 Put the bowl of flour on a damp folded tea towel to stop the bowl moving. **Gradually whisk the milk mixture into the flour** and keep whisking until it is smooth. Cover the bowl with plastic wrap and put it in the refrigerator for 30 minutes.

5 Put about ¹/₂ teaspoon of the butter in a medium frying pan on the stove and turn the heat to medium. Fill a ¹/₄ cup measure with the milk and flour mixture (batter). When the butter is melted, **pour the batter into the pan.**

6 Cook the hotcake for about 2 minutes or **until it is just set around the edge and small bubbles have burst on the surface.** Using an egg slide, turn the hotcake over and cook it for another 2 minutes or until the other side is lightly browned. Take the hotcake out of the pan and place it on a serving plate (you can stack the hotcakes until you're ready to eat). Cook the rest of the batter in the same way using the rest of the butter.

Topping them off

Bananas with maple syrup
Top the hotcakes with sliced bananas then drizzle maple syrup over them.

Lemon, butter and sugar
Put a dob of butter on each hotcake, pour some lemon juice over and sprinkle with sugar.

Nutty berry treat
Spread the hotcakes with Nutella and scatter over a few sliced fresh strawberries.

super scrambled eggs

It is important to use oven mitts when cooking in a microwave oven as some dishes can get hot.
We have served our scrambled eggs on English muffins but you can also use toast or bagels.

ingredients

6 eggs

$^1/_2$ cup milk

2 tablespoons chopped fresh chives

30g butter

4 English muffins

★ Serves 4

Using the microwave oven

1 Break the eggs into a medium bowl, add the milk and chives then whisk until mixed together. Put the butter in a shallow microwave-safe dish. Put the dish in the microwave oven, without a lid, and cook on HIGH (100%) for about 20-seconds or until the butter is melted. **Using oven mitts, take the dish out of the microwave oven.**

2 **Pour the egg mixture** into the dish.

3 Return the dish to the microwave oven and cook the egg mixture, without a lid, on HIGH (100%) for 1 minute.

Take the dish out of the oven and **stir the egg mixture with a wooden spoon.** Repeat the cooking and stirring 2 more times so the eggs have been cooked for a total of 3 minutes. If the eggs are not set enough for you, then cook on HIGH (100%) for another 30 seconds.

While the eggs are cooking, split the muffins and toast them in a toaster or under a heated grill until lightly browned. Serve the eggs on the muffins.

Using the stove

1 Break the eggs into a medium bowl, add the milk and chives then **whisk until mixed together.**

2 **Put the butter in a medium saucepan on the stove** and turn the heat to medium. When the butter is melted, turn the heat to low.

3 Pour the egg mixture into the pan and cook it, without stirring, until it begins to set around the edge. **Using a wooden spoon, gently stir the egg mixture** until it looks firm but is still a bit creamy.

Before you start eating, fill the pan or dish with cold water as this will make it easier to clean.

Scrambled eggs

French toast

Serve the French toast as soon as it is ready or the crispy crust will go soggy. It's fun to make French toast in different shapes—just use different shaped biscuit cutters. You could serve trees at Christmas, cats at Halloween or bunnies at Easter.

ingredients

4 thick slices white bread

1 egg

1 tablespoon water

2 tablespoons caster sugar

30g butter

1/4 teaspoon ground cinnamon

★ *Makes 4*

1 Put the bread on a chopping board then use a round biscuit cutter that is about 9cm across to **cut a piece from each bread slice.** Or you can just cut off the crusts.

2 Break the egg into a small bowl, add the water and 2 teaspoons of the sugar, then **beat with a fork until mixed together.**

3 **Put the butter in a medium frying pan on the stove** and turn the heat to medium.

4 When the butter is melted, **dip the bread rounds quickly into the egg mixture,** 1 at a time. Let the extra mixture run off the bread then carefully place the bread in the pan. (Place the bowl with the egg mixture in it near the stove so you can pop each bread round into the pan as soon as you have dipped it.)

5 Cook the bread rounds for about 2-minutes or until they are lightly browned underneath. Using an egg slide, turn the French toast over and lightly brown the other side. **Remove the French toast from the pan and put it on a tray covered with kitchen paper.**

6 Use your fingers to mix the rest of the sugar and the cinnamon together in a small bowl. **Sprinkle both sides of the French toast with the sugar mixture.**

egg and bacon muffins

ingredients

4 bacon rashers

vegetable oil,
   for brushing egg rings

30g butter

4 eggs

4 English muffins

40g butter, extra

4 cheese slices

★ *Makes 4*

1 Put the bacon on a chopping board. **Using kitchen scissors, cut the rind from the bacon** then cut the bacon in half.

2 Put a medium frying pan on the stove and turn the heat to high. Put all the bacon in the pan and cook it for 2-minutes or until it is lightly browned on 1 side. Using tongs, turn the bacon over and cook it for another 2 minutes or until the other side is browned. **Take the bacon out of the pan and put it on a plate covered with kitchen paper.** Cover the bacon with foil to keep it warm while you're cooking the eggs.

3 **Brush the inside of 4 egg rings with a little vegetable oil.**

4 Put the butter in the same pan and turn the heat to medium. When the butter is melted, put the 4 egg rings in the pan. **Break 1 egg into a small jug then pour it into an egg ring.** Do the same with the rest of the eggs.

5 Cover the pan with a lid, turn the heat to low, and **cook the eggs until the whites are set and the yolks are as you like them.**

We used a frying pan with a lid for this recipe. If you don't have a lid, just cover the pan with a flat oven tray but be sure to wear oven mitts when removing the tray so you don't burn yourself.

6 While the eggs are cooking, **split the muffins and cook them in a toaster** or under a heated grill until lightly browned. Spread the muffins with the extra butter.

7 Using tongs, lift the egg rings from the eggs. Put 2 pieces of the bacon on half a muffin. Using an egg slide, lift an egg out of the pan and put it on the bacon. **Put a slice of cheese on the egg** then top with the other half of the muffin. Stack the rest of the muffins, bacon, eggs and cheese in the same way.

Using the microwave oven

It's easy to cook bacon in the microwave oven. Just put it between 2 pieces of kitchen paper in a single layer on a microwave-safe plate and cook on HIGH (100%) for about 2 minutes for every rasher you use.

boiled eggs and hash browns

Cold eggs will crack when they are cooking, so it's best to use eggs which have not been in the refrigerator.

ingredients

4 eggs

★ *Makes 4*

Boiled eggs

1 Put the eggs in a medium saucepan on the stove. **Use a jug to pour in enough cold water to just cover the eggs.** Put the lid on. Turn the heat to high.

2 **Bring the water to the boil.** Set the timer and boil the eggs, without a lid, for 3 minutes for soft-boiled or 6 minutes for hard-boiled. Turn the stove off, take the pan off the stove and place it on a wooden board.

3 **Using a metal spoon, take the eggs from the pan** and put each egg in an egg cup. Empty the pan.

4 Use a dry tea towel to hold the egg. Tap the side of the egg with a teaspoon to lightly **crack the shell then use the spoon to cut the top off.** Serve soft-boiled eggs with hot buttered toast for dipping.

5 To peel hard-boiled eggs, return the eggs to the empty pan, cover them with cold water,

Boiled egg

and leave them for 10 minutes. Then take the eggs out of the water and **tap them on a bench to crack the shell.** Gently peel the shell away

from the egg. Wash the eggs gently under cold water to remove any small pieces of shell then pat them dry with kitchen paper.

Eat the hash browns straightaway while they are still crisp, otherwise they'll become soggy.

ingredients

3 medium potatoes

1 egg

$1/2$ cup finely grated cheddar cheese

$1 1/2$ tablespoons plain flour

$1/2$ teaspoon salt

vegetable oil, for
  shallow-frying (see page 8)

★ Makes 6

Hash browns

Hash browns

1 Turn the oven to 160°C. Peel and grate the potatoes on the largest holes of the grater. Put the potatoes in a strainer over a large bowl. **Squeeze any extra liquid out of the potato with your hands.** They will start to go pink, but keep going—it's okay.

2 Crack the egg into a medium bowl and beat it with a fork. **Add the potato, cheese, flour and salt and mix together.**

3 Put a medium frying pan on the stove, turn the heat to high, and put the oil in the pan. Wait 1 minute, then turn the heat to medium. Fill a $1/4$-cup measure with some of the potato mixture. **Carefully empty the mixture into the pan** and flatten it with an egg slide.

4 **Fry the hash brown until it is lightly browned around the edge—lift it with the egg slide to check.** Using an egg slide, turn the hash brown over and cook it for another 2 minutes

or until the other side is lightly browned. Lift the hash brown from the pan and put it on an oven tray covered with kitchen paper. Cook the rest of the potato mixture in the same way. Keep the hash browns warm by placing them in a low oven, while you cook the rest.

Don't cover the hash browns or they will go soggy. After you have cooked 1 or 2 hash browns, try cooking more than 1 at a time if the pan is big enough.

perfect porridge

We have suggested serving brown sugar or honey with the porridge, but drizzling over a little golden syrup is a great Australian favourite.

ingredients

1¹/₃ cups water

¹/₂ cup rolled oats

milk

honey or brown sugar

some chopped fresh strawberries

★ Serves 1 or 2

1 **Put the water and oats in a medium saucepan** on the stove, and turn the heat to medium. Stir thwe mixture with a wooden spoon until it boils.

2 Turn the heat a little lower to stop the porridge boiling over the side of the pan. **Stir the porridge for about 4 minutes or until it is thick and creamy.** Spoon the porridge into serving bowls, pour over as much milk as you like, drizzle over some honey or sprinkle with brown sugar, and top with strawberries.

Using the microwave oven

Here is a quick way to cook porridge. Mix the oats and water together in a microwave-safe serving bowl. Put the bowl in the microwave oven without a lid and cook on HIGH (100%) for 1 minute. The porridge will puff up—be careful as it will be very hot. Using oven mitts, remove the dish and stir well. Return the dish to the microwave oven and cook the porridge for 1-minute more or until the porridge is thick and creamy.

Perfect porridge

mouth-watering
waffles

The strawberry rhubarb topping is also great served on top of porridge or any other cereal. It will keep, covered, for a week in the refrigerator.

ingredients

250g strawberries

200g (about 3 stalks) rhubarb

$1/2$ cup caster sugar

12 frozen waffles

2 tablespoons flaked almonds, toasted

★ Serves 4 or 6

1 Cut the tops from the strawberries and cut each strawberry in half. **Cut the rhubarb into small pieces about 2cm long.**

2 Put a medium saucepan on the stove. Put the strawberries, rhubarb and sugar in the pan and turn the heat to low. **Stir the mixture until the sugar is dissolved.** Turn the heat to medium and simmer (which means the water is bubbling gently) for 10 minutes until the mixture is thickened.

Meanwhile cook the waffles in a toaster until crisp. Then serve the waffles with the strawberry rhubarb topping and sprinkle the almonds on top.

Waffles with strawberry rhubarb topping

the wedge

ingredients

Potato wedges

4 medium potatoes, unpeeled

1 tablespoon olive oil

1 tablespoon chicken seasoning

cooking-oil spray

★ *Makes 24*

Start making the wedges about 1 hour before you're ready to eat them. The salsa and dips can be made while the potatoes are cooking.

1 Turn the oven to 230°C. **Wash and scrub the potatoes well,** and dry them with kitchen paper.

2 Cut the potatoes in half on a chopping board. **Cut each half into wedges.**

3 Put the wedges in a medium bowl with the oil and the chicken seasoning, **and mix well.**

4 Lightly spray a baking dish with cooking-oil spray. **Put the wedges in the dish.** Bake, uncovered, in the oven for 40-minutes or until they are browned lightly.

Serve the wedges with any of the dips we show on the right.

ingredients

Creamy avocado dip

2 medium avocados

1/4 cup bottled ranch dressing

1 tablespoon lemon juice

Cut the avocados in half lengthways (cutting around the seed) then twist the halves to separate them from the seed. Use a spoon to scoop out the seed, then scoop the avocado into the bowl of a food processor. **Add the ranch dressing and lemon juice,** then process until smooth.

If you can't find ranch dressing, use coleslaw dressing instead.

ingredients

Chilli dip

1 cup sour cream

1/4 cup bottled sweet chilli sauce

Put both ingredients in a medium bowl and **mix together with a spoon.**

Chilli dip

SARA

ingredients

Mexican corn salsa

130g can corn kernels, drained

375g jar mild chunky salsa

1 teaspoon ground cumin

2 teaspoons dried parsley flakes

Tip the corn into a strainer over the sink to drain away the liquid. **Put the corn in a medium bowl with the salsa, cumin and parsley,** and mix together with a spoon.

Mexican corn salsa

ingredients

Mixed salad

1 Lebanese cucumber

250g cherry tomatoes

1 medium carrot

8 cos lettuce leaves

1 medium avocado

Salad dressing

$1/2$ cup vegetable oil

$1/4$ cup lemon juice

1 teaspoon Dijon mustard

2 teaspoons sugar

★   Serves 4

Mixed salad

super salads

You should make the salad just before you're ready to eat it, but the salad dressing can be made ahead of time. Keep it in a glass jar, with the lid on, in the refrigerator.

1 Slice the cucumber and cut the tomatoes in half on a chopping board. Peel the carrot and cut it into thick sticks. Tear the lettuce into bite-sized pieces. Cut the avocado in half lengthways (cutting around the seed), then twist the halves to separate them from the seed. Scoop out the seed with a spoon and carefully peel the skin away from the avocado. **Cut the avocado into slices.** Place the lettuce, carrot, cucumber, tomatoes and avocado into a large salad bowl.

2 Salad dressing
Put all the ingredients in a glass jar. **Screw the lid on tightly and shake well.** Drizzle the dressing over the salad and toss it together with salad servers.

Salad spinners make it easy to wash and dry lettuce leaves properly.

ingredients

*Creamy potato
and crispy bacon salad*

1kg baby potatoes

2 bacon rashers

2 medium onions

1 tablespoon olive oil

$^1/_3$ cup chopped
   fresh parsley

Dressing

$^1/_2$ cup bottled
French dressing

$^1/_2$ cup sour cream

40g packet French
   onion soup mix

★ *Serves 6*

*Creamy potato and crispy
bacon salad*

1 **Cut the potatoes in half on a chopping board.** Put a large saucepan on the stove, put the potatoes in the pan, and use a jug to pour in just enough water to cover the potatoes. Turn the heat to high, cover the pan with a lid, and bring the water to the boil. Simmer the potatoes for 7-minutes or until they are just soft when you pierce one with a fork. Stand a large strainer in the sink. Using oven mitts, take the pan to the sink and pour the potatoes into the strainer. Run some cold water over the potatoes and let the water drain away. Leave the potatoes to cool for $^1/_2$ hour.

This salad is made with cold potatoes, so you will need to cook them about $^1/_2$ hour before you are going to eat.

2 While the potatoes are boiling, use kitchen scissors to cut the rind from the bacon, then cut the bacon into small pieces. Chop the onions on a chopping board. Put a large frying pan on the stove, turn the heat to medium, and put the oil in the pan. Wait 30 seconds, **then add the bacon and onion and stir until the onion is soft.**

3 **Dressing**
Mix together the French dressing, sour cream and the dry French onion soup mix in a small bowl. Cover the bowl and let the mixture stand for 30-minutes to soften the soup mix. Put the potatoes, bacon mixture and parsley in a large bowl, **spoon over the Dressing** and gently mix together. Transfer to a salad bowl to serve.

chicken noodle soup

You can buy liquid chicken stock in packs or you can make it up by adding water to stock cubes or powder.

ingredients

130g can corn kernels

2 chicken breast fillets

1½ cups chicken stock

2 cups water

1 teaspoon soy sauce

85g packet
chicken-flavoured
2-minute noodles

10 chives

★ *Serves 2 to 4*

1 Pour the corn into a strainer over the sink to drain. **Cut the chicken into 1cm wide strips on a chopping board.**

2 Put a medium saucepan on the stove. Pour in the stock and water and turn the heat to high. Put the lid on. Bring the stock to the boil. **Add the chicken, corn, soy sauce, the chicken-flavour sachet from the noodles and the noodles to the pan.** Bring the soup back to the boil, turn the heat to medium and cook for 2 minutes. Turn the heat off.

3 When the soup stops boiling, **use kitchen scissors to cut the chives into the soup.** Use a ladle to divide the soup among soup bowls.

Chicken noodle soup

snack attack

You can use any sandwich bread for these snacks—the choice is yours. Eat them while they are still hot and crunchy.

Egg and cheese snack

Beetroot, carrot and pineapple snack

Spaghetti and cheese snack

ingredients

Spaghetti and cheese filling

130g can spaghetti with
  cheese and tomato

2 cheese slices

★ Serves 2

ingredients

Beetroot, carrot and pineapple filling

4 slices canned beetroot, drained

2 slices pineapple thins, drained

1/4 cup grated carrot

2 mozzarella cheese slices

★ Serves 2

ingredients

Egg and cheese snacks

4 slices bread

soft butter

2 small eggs

2 cheese slices

★ *Serves 2*

Egg and cheese snacks

1 Turn on the electric snack-maker, making sure the lid is closed. **Spread 1 side of each slice of the bread with some butter.**

2 When the snack-maker is hot, open the lid and place 2 slices of the bread, buttered-side down, in the snack-maker. **Gently push down on the bread with a spoon to make a hollow.**

3 Break 1 egg into a small jug and **pour the egg into the hollow in the bread.** Do the same thing with the other egg and the other piece of bread.

4 **Put a slice of cheese on top of each egg.**

5 **Cover the cheese with the other 2 slices of the bread, buttered-side up.** Close the snack-maker firmly. Cook the snack for about 3-minutes or until browned.

6 Turn the power off. **Open the snack-maker** and use tongs to carefully remove the snacks.

Don't stop there!

Try the other tasty fillings on the other page, following the same method. Have you ever thought of making sweet snacks for dessert? They make really quick and easy "pies". Try 1 cup milk chocolate Melts with 2-tablespoons hundreds and thousands; or 2 tablespoons peanut butter with 2 tablespoons honey. Even 1 cup of canned pie fruit tastes great.

ultra smoothies

ingredients

Fruit tango smoothie

1 medium mango

1 medium banana

2 strawberries

200g tub honey and
vanilla yogurt

1 cup milk

10 ice cubes

2 teaspoons honey

1 scoop vanilla ice-cream

2 passionfruit

★ *Makes 4 cups*

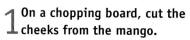

1 **On a chopping board, cut the cheeks from the mango.**

2 **Cut the flesh from around the mango stone.**

3 **Using a spoon, scoop the flesh from the mango cheeks** and put all the mango in a blender. Chop the banana and cut the tops off the strawberries. Put the banana, strawberries, yogurt, milk, ice, honey and ice-cream in the blender, put the lid on, and blend until the mixture is smooth. Remove the lid. Turn the power off.

4 Cut the passionfruit in half. **Using a small spoon, scoop out the passionfruit pulp, add it to the smoothie,** and stir until mixed together.

The flavour of your smoothie will change with the ripeness of the fruit. Use overripe bananas for a sweeter taste. Many different fruits can be used to change the flavour of a smoothie.

ingredients

Malted banana smoothie

2 medium bananas

1 cup milk

1/4 cup malted
  milk powder

1 tablespoon honey

8 ice cubes

1 scoop vanilla
  ice-cream

★ *Makes 3 cups*

*Malted banana smoothie (left)
with Fruit tango smoothie*

1 **Cut up the bananas on a chopping board.**

2 **Put all the ingredients into a blender,** put the lid on then blend until the mixture is smooth.

pumpkin soup

You can make the pumpkin soup a day before you want to eat it. But, if you do, don't add the cream until after you've reheated the soup just before you're ready to eat.

ingredients

750g piece butternut pumpkin

1 medium onion

2 bacon rashers

1 tablespoon butter

3 1/2 cups water

1 chicken stock cube

1/4 cup cream

★ Serves 4

1 On a chopping board, scoop out the pumpkin seeds with a spoon **then carefully peel the pumpkin with a sharp knife.** (You may need to get an adult to help you do this.) Cut the pumpkin into pieces which are about 4cm square. Chop the onion. Using kitchen scissors, cut the rind from the bacon, then cut the bacon into small pieces.

2 Put the butter in a large saucepan on the stove and turn the heat to medium. When the butter is melted, **add the onion and the bacon, and stir until the onion is soft.**

Pumpkin soup

3 **Add the pumpkin, water and crumbled stock cube to the pan.** Put the lid on the pan, turn the heat to high, and bring to the boil.

4 Remove the lid, turn the heat to low and simmer (which means the liquid is bubbling gently) for 30 minutes or until the pumpkin is cooked. **Put a knife in the pumpkin to see if it is cooked**—it should be just soft.

5 Turn the stove off and leave the pumpkin mixture to cool for 10 minutes. **Using a ladle, put some of the soup into the bowl of a food processor so that the bowl is about 1/3 full.** Process the soup until it is smooth. Put a clean saucepan on the stove and put the smooth mixture into the pan. Keep processing the soup in small batches until all the mixture is smooth.

6 **Stir in the cream, turn the heat to medium and stir the soup until it is hot.** If you like, drizzle another tablespoon of cream into each bowl. You can make a face or perhaps your initials.

Serve the pumpkin soup with crusty bread.

ingredients

Chicken and avocado sandwiches

$^1/_2$ small avocado

1 tablespoon sour cream

1 teaspoon lemon juice

4 slices bread

2 tablespoons mayonnaise

$^1/_2$ cup chopped cooked chicken

★   *Makes 2*

1 Scoop the flesh from the avocado with a spoon, put it into a small bowl, then **using a fork, mash the avocado with the sour cream and lemon juice.**

2 Spread 1 side of 2 of the bread slices with the avocado mixture. **Spread 1 side of the remaining 2 bread slices with the mayonnaise.**

3 **Put the chicken on top of the bread slices with the mayonnaise.** Top the chicken with the bread slices covered in avocado.

lunch-box specials

Choose your favourite bread and either barbecue chicken or leftover roast chicken to make these sandwiches.

Chicken and avocado sandwiches

ingredients

Ham salad pitta

2 lettuce leaves

1 medium carrot

1 small tomato

2 small pitta pocket bread

2 tablespoons mayonnaise

2 slices ham

1/4 cup grated cheddar cheese

★ *Makes 2*

Ham salad pitta

1 Shred the lettuce leaves on a chopping board, grate the carrot, and cut the tomato in half then slice it. **Cut a 10cm slit along the join of both pieces of the pitta.** Spread the inside of each pocket with the mayonnaise.

2 **Fill each pocket with the lettuce, tomato, ham, cheese and carrot.**

ingredients

Salami, cheese and tomato bread stick

1 small French bread stick (about 35cm long)

soft butter

1 medium tomato

4 slices mild salami

1/2 cup grated cheddar cheese

4 lettuce leaves

★ *Makes 2*

1 Cut the bread stick into 2 pieces. **Cut each piece not quite all the way through so the two halves are still joined.** Spread the insides with some butter.

2 Slice the tomato on a chopping board. Fill the bread sticks by overlapping the tomato and the salami, **then top with the cheese and lettuce.**

Salami, cheese and tomato bread stick

ingredients

Banana and peanut butter roll-ups

2 medium bananas

1 tablespoon lemon juice

2 pieces lavash or
   mountain bread

$1/3$ cup crunchy peanut butter

1 tablespoon honey

★   *Makes 2*

1 Slice the bananas on a chopping board and **put them in a small bowl with the lemon juice.** Toss them gently with a metal spoon so the banana is coated with the lemon juice.

2 Spread 1 side of each piece of bread with the peanut butter, **then put the banana on top.**

3 **Drizzle the honey over the banana,** then roll up the bread.

It is great fun—and less mess— to use squeeze bottles of honey to make these roll-ups.

Banana and peanut butter roll-ups

stuffed spuds

ingredients

Stuffed spuds

4 large potatoes, unpeeled
vegetable oil

★ *Serves 4*

Start these about an hour ahead to give them enough time to bake. Choose a variation from the next page or fill them with your favourite filling. You can use the leftover potato flesh for potato salad or bubble and squeak.

1 Turn the oven to 180°C. Wash and scrub the potatoes well, and dry them with kitchen paper. **Pierce the potato skin in about 5 places with a fork.**

2 Brush a baking dish with the oil. Put the potatoes in the dish and bake, uncovered, in the oven for 1 hour. Turn the oven off. Using oven mitts, take the dish out of the oven and put it on a wooden board. **Test the potatoes with a skewer to make sure they are soft.**

3 Hold a potato with an oven mitt on a chopping board and **cut off 1 long side. Do the same thing with the rest of the potatoes.**

4 **Use a metal spoon to gently scoop out the middle of the potatoes.** Fill the potato shells with your chosen filling. Then sprinkle chopped herbs over the top to make them look interesting.

ingredients

Beans 'n' cheese filling

3 x 215g cans baked beans

1/3 cup finely grated
cheddar cheese

Turn the oven to 200°C. Spoon
the beans into the potato cases.
Sprinkle the cheese over the top.
Put the potatoes on an oven tray
and bake them, uncovered, in the
oven for 10 minutes or until the
cheese is melted.

Beans 'n' cheese filling

Using the microwave oven

Wash and scrub the potatoes (don't
dry them as they need to be moist
when they go into the microwave
oven). Pierce the potato skin in about
5-places with a fork. Put the potatoes
onto a microwave-safe flat plate, or on
the turntable in the microwave oven.
Cook on HIGH (100%) for 5-minutes.

Using tongs, turn the potatoes over.
Cook on HIGH (100%) for another
5-minutes. Test the potatoes with a
skewer to make sure they are soft. Take
the potatoes out of the microwave
oven with an oven mitt as they will be
very hot. Finish the potatoes following
Steps 3 and 4 (page 39).

ingredients

Creamy tuna and celery filling

1 stick celery

125g cream cheese, chopped, softened

180g can tuna in brine, drained

1/2 cup sour cream

Cut the celery into 10cm lengths on a chopping board. Cut the 10cm lengths into thin strips then chop them into small pieces.

Put the cream cheese in a small bowl and beat it with a wooden spoon until it is smooth. Stir the celery, tuna and sour cream into the cheese until mixed together.

Take the cream cheese out of the refrigerator about 30 minutes before you want to use it so it is soft.

Avocado, bacon and cottage cheese filling

ingredients

Avocado, bacon and cottage cheese filling

4 bacon rashers

1 small avocado

3/4 cup cottage cheese

Using kitchen scissors, cut the rind from the bacon then cut the bacon into small pieces.

Put a small frying pan on the stove and turn the heat to high. Put the bacon in the pan and cook, stirring, until the bacon is well browned. Remove the bacon from the pan and put it on a plate covered with kitchen paper.

Cut the avocado in half lengthways (cutting around the seed) then twist the halves to separate them from the seed. Use a spoon to scoop out the seed then scoop the avocado flesh into a small bowl. Mash the avocado with a fork until smooth. Stir in the bacon and cottage cheese.

Creamy tuna and celery filling

Omelettes can be varied in many ways. Try adding herbs such as parsley to the egg mixture before you cook it, or add some chopped ham to the cheese when you sprinkle it over the top.

ingredients

2 eggs

1 tablespoon water

2 teaspoons butter

1/4 cup grated
   cheddar cheese

★ *Serves 1*

cheese omelette

1 **Break the eggs into a small jug.** Add the water then beat with a fork until mixed together.

2 Put the butter in a medium frying pan on the stove and turn the heat to high. When the butter is melted, tilt the pan to cover the base and halfway up the side with the butter. **Pour the egg mixture into the pan.**

2

4 Continue cooking the omelette until the egg mixture is nearly set. The top should still look creamy. **Sprinkle the cheese over the top.**

5 Hold the pan with one hand; with the other hand, **use an egg slide to fold the omelette in half.**

6 Still using the oven mitt to hold the pan, **slide the omelette onto a serving plate.**

3

5

6

3 When the egg starts to set, tilt the pan and, **using a wooden spoon, push the edge of the omelette from the side of the pan.** This will let the uncooked egg run under the cooked egg and onto the hot pan so it will cook too.

Cheese omelette

fabulous fettuccine

This dish will be popular with all the family. There is not too much work to do beforehand and you can use any kind of dried pasta—just check the packet to see how long you should cook it.

ingredients

1 large onion

2 cloves garlic

250g button mushrooms

4 bacon rashers

375g dried fettuccine

2 tablespoons olive oil

300ml cream

★ Serves 4 to 6

1 Cut the onion in half then slice it, crush the garlic and slice the mushrooms. Put the bacon on a chopping board. **Using kitchen scissors, cut the rind from the bacon** then cut the bacon into thin pieces.

2 Put a large saucepan on the stove. Use a jug to pour in enough water to come 3/4 of the way up the side of the pan. Turn the heat to high, cover the pan with a lid and bring the water to the boil. **Using oven mitts, remove the lid and add the fettuccine to the boiling water.** When the water boils again, stir the fettuccine with a wooden spoon.

Creamy bacon and mushroom fettuccine

3 While the fettuccine is cooking, put a large frying pan on the stove, turn the heat to medium and put the oil in the pan. Add the onion, garlic and bacon, and stir until the onion is soft. **Add the mushrooms** and stir until they are soft.

4 **Add the cream to the mushroom mixture** and cook for 5 minutes.

5 **Test the fettuccine by taking a couple of strands from the pan with some tongs,** letting it cool slightly then tasting it. If it is just soft, it is ready. Stand a large strainer in the sink. Using oven mitts take the pan of fettuccine to the sink and pour it into the strainer. Let the water drain away.

Serve the bacon and mushroom sauce over the fettuccine.

oriental
beef with rice

ingredients

2^1/$_2$ cups water

1^1/$_2$ cups long-grain rice

2 medium onions

2 large carrots

2 cloves garlic

2 tablespoons vegetable oil

2 cups broccoli pieces

3 teaspoons cornflour

^{1}/$_2$ cup water, extra

^{1}/$_4$ cup honey

^{1}/$_4$ cup soy sauce

^{1}/$_2$ teaspoon beef
   stock powder

1 teaspoon sesame oil

500g beef strips

★ Serves 4 to 6

There are lots of vegetables to chop for this
recipe, so start preparing the dish about
^{3}/$_4$ hour before you plan to eat.

1 Put a medium saucepan on the stove. Put the water then the rice in the pan. **Turn the heat to high then, when the water is boiling, turn the heat to low.** Put a tight-fitting lid on the pan then simmer for 12 minutes. Turn the stove off, leave the pan on the stove with the lid on. After 5-minutes, remove the lid and lightly stir the rice with a fork.

2 While the rice is cooking, cut the onions in half on a chopping board. **Cut each half into wedges.** Slice the carrots into thin rounds then, if you like, cut each carrot round in half. Crush the garlic.

3 Put a large wok on the stove, turn the heat to high and put half the vegetable oil in the wok. Wait 30 seconds then put the onion, carrot and garlic in the wok. **Stir-fry the vegetables with a wooden spatula or a wooden spoon** until the onions are soft.

4 **Add the broccoli then stir-fry with a wooden spatula for 2 more minutes.**

5 Using oven mitts, take the wok from the stove and place it on a wooden board. **Spoon the vegetable mixture into a large bowl.** Put

the cornflour into a medium jug, stir in the extra water then stir in the honey, soy sauce, stock powder and sesame oil until mixed together.

6 Return the wok to the stove, turn the heat to high and add the rest of the vegetable oil. **Wait 30 seconds then put half the beef strips into the wok and stir-fry with a wooden spatula until the beef is lightly browned all over.** Take the beef out of the wok and put it on a plate. Stir-fry the rest of the beef in the same way. Return all the beef to the wok. Keep the heat on high.

7 Give the honey mixture a good stir then pour it over the beef in the wok and **stir with a wooden spatula until the sauce boils and thickens slightly.** Return the vegetable mixture to the wok and stir with a wooden spatula until everything is hot.

Serve the beef and vegetables with the steamed rice.

If you can't get beef strips from the butcher, you can use any boneless beef that is suitable for stir-frying.

Oriental beef with rice

Start making the ribs about 1 hour before you're ready to eat. They can be put into the sauce mixture (marinade) overnight for more flavour. When marinating the ribs, cover them tightly with plastic wrap and put them in the refrigerator.

finger lickin'

ingredients

Ribs

1 tablespoon honey

2 tablespoons plum sauce

1 tablespoon barbecue sauce

1 tablespoon tomato sauce

2 teaspoons soy sauce

2 racks (600g) American-style
   pork ribs

Steamed corn cobs

2 large corn cobs

40g butter

★　*Serves 2*

1 Turn the oven to 200°C. **Put the honey and all the sauces into a large glass bowl** then stir to mix together.

2 **Put 1 rack of ribs in the bowl, turning it with your hands so it gets covered in the sauce mixture.**

3 **Put a metal rack in a baking dish and sit the coated ribs on it.** Repeat Step 2 for the second rack of ribs. Leave the leftover sauce mixture in the bowl for later. Put the ribs in the oven and bake, uncovered, for 30 minutes. Remove the ribs from the oven and brush them with the rest of the sauce mixture. Put the ribs back into the oven for about 20 minutes or until cooked.

4 Remove the husk and silk (the hairy bits between the husk and the cob) from the cobs.

5 Cut off the ends of the corn on a chopping board.

6 Put a steamer in a medium saucepan on the stove. **Pour about 1 cup of water into the pan (make sure the water is not touching the base of the steamer),** turn the heat to high and bring the water to the boil. Using tongs, put the corn into the steamer and cover the pan with a lid. Turn the heat to low, and steam for about 10 minutes or until the corn is tender.

7 To test the corn, turn the stove off and carefully remove the lid. **Use a fork to pierce the corn just once to see if the kernels are tender.** Using tongs, put the corn on a chopping board and cut each cob in half. Using tongs, put the corn onto serving plates and top with the butter. Cut each rack of ribs in half and put on the same plate with the corn.

A steamer is a round metal or bamboo basket with holes which allow steam from the simmering water to cook the food.

Using the microwave oven

Complete Steps 4 and 5 then put 2 tablespoons of water into a shallow microwave-safe dish. Add the corn, cover with microwave-safe plastic wrap. Put the dish in the microwave oven and cook on HIGH (100%) for 4 minutes. Being careful not to burn yourself, remove the plastic wrap (steam builds up under the wrap). Complete Step 7. If the corn is not cooked through, replace the plastic wrap and cook on HIGH (100%) for about 1 more minute or until the corn is cooked.

ribs and corn

Finger lickin' ribs and corn

mexican
munchies

Eat nachos as soon as they are ready or the corn chips will go soggy. The Mexibeans used in this recipe come in a can and are red kidney beans with capsicum, tomato pieces and spices added. If you can't get them, use plain kidney beans and a small amount of bottled chilli sauce.

ingredients

Vegie nachos

1 medium onion

1 clove garlic

1 tablespoon olive oil

425g can chopped tomatoes

420g can Mexibeans

240g packet corn chips

1 cup grated cheese

1 large avocado

1/2 cup sour cream

1 tablespoon lemon juice

★ *Serves 4*

1 Turn the oven to 200°C. Chop the onion on a chopping board and crush the garlic. Put a medium saucepan on the stove, turn the heat to medium, and put the oil in the pan. Wait 30 seconds then add the onion and garlic. Stir until the onion is soft. Add the tomatoes with their juice then **add the beans and stir to mix together.**

2 Simmer the bean mixture, without a lid, for 15 minutes, **stirring often until the mixture thickens slightly.**

1

2

3

4

Vegie nachos

3 Put the corn chips onto a large ovenproof plate, **pour the bean mixture over the corn chips** and sprinkle with the cheese. Put the nachos in the oven and bake, uncovered, for 10 minutes or until the cheese is melted.

4 While the nachos are cooking, cut the avocado in half lengthways (cutting around the seed). Twist the halves to separate them from the seed. Scoop out the seed with a spoon. Use a spoon to scoop out the avocado flesh and place it in a medium bowl. Add half the sour cream and the lemon juice to the avocado. **Mash with a fork until mixed together.**

To serve, put spoonfuls of the avocado mixture and the rest of the sour cream over the nachos.

Chilli con carne

Use the bolognese sauce recipe (page 56) to make a delicious variation—chilli con carne. When you add the onion and garlic to the saucepan, also put in 1 tablespoon ground cumin and 2 teaspoons sweet paprika. Do not put grated carrot or zucchini in this recipe; instead, drain a 300g can of kidney beans into a medium strainer, rinse the beans under cold water and drain them again before putting them into the pan. Chilli con carne is not served with spaghetti; it is delicious served with a crunchy bread roll and a spoonful of sour cream on top.

Beef tacos are sort of like a Mexican hamburger. You can also make tacos without meat by following Steps 1 and 2 in the nachos recipe.

Beef tacos

ingredients

Beef tacos

8 lettuce leaves

2 medium tomatoes

2 teaspoons olive oil

500g minced beef

1 clove garlic

1$^{1}/_{2}$ cups water

2 tablespoons
   tomato paste

35g packet
   taco seasoning

12 taco shells

1 cup grated cheese

$^{1}/_{2}$ cup bottled mild
   chunky salsa

★ *Makes 12*

1 Turn the oven to 180°C. On a chopping board, roll up the lettuce leaves then using a knife, shred them finely. Chop the tomatoes. Put a large frying pan on the stove, turn the heat to high and put the oil in the pan. Wait for 30 seconds then add the minced beef. **Crush the garlic and add to the pan with the beef.** Stir for about 5 minutes or until the beef is browned all over.

2 **Add the water, tomato paste and taco seasoning** to the beef mixture, then stir to mix together. Simmer, without a lid, for about 10 minutes or until most of the liquid is gone.

3 While the mince mixture is cooking, **put the taco shells upside down on an oven tray.** Put the tray in the oven, uncovered, and bake for 5 minutes. Using oven mitts, take the tray out of the oven and place it on a wooden board, allowing the taco shells to cool for just 1 minute.

4 **Divide the beef mixture among the taco shells,** then top with lettuce, tomato and cheese. Drizzle with the salsa.

peanut chicken skewers and garlic bread

The bamboo skewers used in this recipe are soaked in water first so they will not burn. You can also use metal skewers—these don't need to be soaked but spraying them with a cooking-oil spray helps the chicken slide off easily.

Peanut chicken skewers and garlic bread

ingredients

Peanut chicken skewers

4 chicken thigh fillets

1 small onion

1 clove garlic

1 tablespoon vegetable oil

2 teaspoons ground cumin

$3/4$ cup chicken stock

$1/3$ cup crunchy peanut butter

$1/4$ cup water

1 tablespoon plum sauce

2 teaspoons bottled sweet chilli sauce

2 teaspoons soy sauce

cooking-oil spray

★ Makes 8

1 Soak 8 short bamboo skewers in a dish of water for 30 minutes. On a chopping board, cut the chicken into 3cm pieces. **Thread the chicken onto the bamboo skewers.** Wash the board well. Finely chop the onion and crush the garlic.

2 Put a medium saucepan on the stove, turn the heat to high, and put the oil in the pan. Wait 30 seconds, turn the heat to medium then add the onion, garlic and cumin. **Stir with a wooden spoon until the onion is soft.**

3 Add the stock, peanut butter, water and the sauces to the pan then **whisk the mixture together.** Simmer, without a lid, for about 2-minutes until the sauce thickens slightly.

4 Lightly spray a griddle pan with cooking-oil spray. Put the pan on the stove and turn the heat to high. Wait 2 minutes then put half the skewers on the pan and cook for 5 minutes or until browned on 1 side. **Using tongs, turn the skewers over** and cook for another 3 minutes or until the other side is browned

and the chicken is cooked through. Put the cooked skewers on an oven tray and cover them with foil to keep them warm. Cook the rest of the skewers in the same way.

Peanut chicken skewers

You need to start the garlic bread about 40 minutes before you're ready to eat. You can make the butter mixture a few hours ahead. If you do, keep it tightly covered in the refrigerator and take it out 10 minutes before you want to spread it.

Garlic bread

ingredients

Garlic bread

2 long bread rolls

2 cloves garlic

80g soft butter

★   *Serves 2 to 4*

1 Turn the oven to 200°C. **Split the bread rolls open then cut each roll in half.** Crush the garlic.

2 Put the garlic and butter in a small bowl **then stir to mix together.**

3 **Spread the garlic butter on the inside of the rolls.**

4 **Wrap the rolls in a piece of foil.** Put the garlic bread in the oven and bake for 30 minutes. Using oven mitts, remove the garlic bread from the oven and carefully unwrap the foil (it will be very hot) to serve.

We used hot-dog rolls, but you can use any kind of bread roll for your garlic bread.

If you make the bolognese sauce a day before you want to eat it, the flavour will be better. Cover the saucepan and reheat the sauce. Take the lid off and stir a few times. Cook the spaghetti just before you're ready to sit down to eat.

spaghetti
bolognese

ingredients

1 large onion

1 clove garlic

1 medium carrot

1 small green zucchini

1 tablespoon olive oil

500g minced beef

2 x 425g cans chopped
   tomatoes

1/3 cup tomato paste

1 tablespoon beef stock powder

1 cup water

500g spaghetti

★ *Serves 6*

1 Finely chop the onion on a chopping board, crush the garlic, and finely grate the carrot and zucchini. Put a large saucepan on the stove, turn the heat to medium, and put the oil in the pan. Wait 30 seconds, add the onion and garlic then stir until the onion is soft. **Add the mince then stir with a wooden spoon until the meat is browned all over.**

2 **Add the tomatoes with their juice, the tomato paste, stock powder, water, carrot and zucchini to the pan.**

3 **Stir the bolognese sauce with a wooden spoon to mix together.** Turn the heat to low, simmer the sauce without the lid for about 30 minutes or until it thickens slightly, stir occasionally with a wooden spoon.

4 While the sauce is cooking, put another large saucepan on the stove. Use a jug to pour in enough water to come 3/4 of the way up the side of the pan. Turn the heat to high, cover the pan with a lid and bring the water to the boil. Using oven mitts, remove the lid and **add the spaghetti to the boiling water.** When the water boils again, stir the spaghetti with a wooden spoon.

5 Boil the spaghetti, without the lid, for about 10 minutes or until it is just soft. **Test it by taking a few strands of the spaghetti from the pan with a fork, letting it cool slightly then tasting it.**

6 Stand a large strainer in the sink. **Using oven mitts, take the pan of spaghetti to the sink and pour the spaghetti into the strainer.** Let the water drain away.

Serve the bolognese sauce over the hot spaghetti.

oodles of noodles stir-fry

Stir-fries don't take long to cook but getting the ingredients ready can take some time. Make sure the chicken and vegetables are all cut up and ready to go then measure out the sauces, honey and oil before you begin to cook.

ingredients

2 chicken breast fillets

2 cloves garlic

1 medium red capsicum

100g snow peas

425g can baby corn

500g packet stir-fry noodles

1 tablespoon oyster sauce

1 tablespoon plum sauce

1 tablespoon soy sauce

1 tablespoon honey

2 tablespoons peanut oil

★ *Serves 6*

1 **Cut the chicken into thin strips** on a chopping board, then wash the board well.

2 Crush the garlic. Cut the capsicum in half on a chopping board, remove the seeds and **cut the capsicum into thin strips.**

3 Remove both ends from the snow peas with your fingers. Tip the corn into a strainer over the sink to drain. **Cut each piece of corn in half.**

4 Put the noodles in a large heatproof bowl. **Cover them with boiling water and leave for 1 minute.** Stand a large strainer in the sink. Using oven mitts, take the bowl of noodles to the sink and pour the noodles into the strainer. Let the water drain away. Put the 3 sauces and the honey in a small jug, and stir to mix together.

5 Put a large wok on the stove, turn the heat to high, and put the oil in the wok. Wait 30 seconds, then add the chicken and garlic to the wok. **Stir-fry with a wooden spatula or wooden spoon until the chicken is lightly browned.**

6 **Add the capsicum, corn and snow peas to the wok,** and stir-fry with a wooden spatula for 2 minutes.

7 Put the noodles into the wok, **pour in the sauce mixture** then stir-fry with a wooden spatula for another 2 minutes or until everything is hot.

Oodles of noodles stir-fry

ingredients

4 medium potatoes, unpeeled

2 tablespoons olive oil

6 trimmed lamb cutlets

1 tablespoon plain flour

1 egg

1¹/₂ tablespoons seasoned
  stuffing mix

1¹/₂ tablespoons
  cornflake crumbs

vegetable oil, for
  shallow-frying
  (see page 10)

★ Serves 4 to 6

1 Turn the oven to 200°C.
Wash and scrub the potatoes
well, and dry them with kitchen
paper. Cut each potato in half on
a chopping board. **Cut each half
into wedges.**

2 Brush a baking dish with
some of the olive oil. **Put the
potato wedges in the dish, and
brush them with the rest of
the oil.** Put the dish in
the oven and bake for
25 minutes. Using
oven mitts, take the
dish out of the
oven and place
it on a wooden
board. Turn the
wedges over with
tongs. Put the
wedges back in
the oven and
bake them for
another 25 minutes
or until they are
lightly browned.

*Crunchy cutlets with
potato wedges*

3 While the wedges are cooking, **use a meat mallet to lightly hit the meat of the cutlets until they are even in thickness.** Place the flour and egg in 2 separate shallow bowls. Using a fork, beat the egg until it all becomes the 1 colour. Mix the stuffing mix and cornflake crumbs together in a third bowl.

4 **Coat 1 cutlet in the flour,** then shake off any extra flour.

5 **Dip the cutlet in the egg, then let the extra egg run off.**

6 **Coat the cutlet in the crumb mixture,** then put it on a plate. Repeat steps 4, 5 and 6 with the rest of the cutlets.

7 Put a large frying pan on the stove, turn the heat to high, and put the oil in the pan. Wait for 1 minute, then turn the heat to medium and put half the cutlets in the pan. Cook the cutlets for 3 minutes or until they are browned underneath. **Using tongs, turn the cutlets over and cook them another 3 minutes or until the other side is browned too.** Remove the cutlets from the pan and put them on kitchen paper on an oven tray. Cover them with foil to keep them warm while you cook the rest in the same way.

Serve the cutlets and the potato wedges with some salad if you wish.

crunchy cutlets
with potato wedges

You need to start the wedges about 1 hour before you're ready to eat them but you can cook the cutlets while the wedges are in the oven.

ingredients

2 cloves garlic

5cm piece fresh ginger

1/3 cup soy sauce

1/3 cup honey

2 tablespoons water

1 teaspoon sesame oil

12 chicken drumsticks

★ Serves 4 to 6

You need to start the honeyed drumsticks about 1 hour before you want to eat them.

1 Turn the oven to 180°C. Crush the garlic. **Put the ginger on a chopping board and carefully cut off the skin.**

2 **Pierce the ginger with a fork and grate it on the medium side of a grater.** Brush the inside of the grater with a pastry brush to help remove the ginger.

3 In a large shallow ovenproof dish, **mix together the garlic, ginger, soy, honey, water and sesame oil with a wooden spoon.**

4 Put the drumsticks in the dish and, **using tongs, turn them over to coat with the sauce mixture.** Put the dish in the oven and bake, uncovered, for 40-minutes or until the drumsticks are cooked through.

These drumsticks are yummy served cold with a salad and potato crisps for a great picnic lunch.

honeyed
drumsticks

Honeyed drumsticks

pizza
express

Ham and pineapple pizza

Pizzas can be put together about 1 hour before you cook them. Cover them and put them in the refrigerator until you are ready to start cooking. You can buy pre-packaged pizza cheese that is a combination of grated cheddar, mozzarella and parmesan cheeses.

ingredients

Ham and pineapple pizza

150g sliced ham

450g can pineapple pieces

1 packaged pizza base
   (about 27cm across)

1/4 cup tomato paste

2/3 cup grated cheese

★ *Serves 2 to 4*

1 Turn the oven to 230°C. **Cut the ham into thin strips on a chopping board.** Tip the pineapple into a strainer over a medium bowl (keep the juice to drink or make ice blocks). Mix the ham and pineapple together in a small bowl.

2 Put the pizza base on a pizza tray or large oven tray. **Spread the tomato paste over the top of the pizza base with a spoon.**

3 Sprinkle half the cheese over the pizza. **Sprinkle the ham and pineapple on top,** then finish with the rest of the cheese. Put the pizza in the oven and bake for 15 minutes or until the cheese is melted and the edge is crisp.

ingredients

Bolognese pizza

100g button mushrooms, sliced

1 tablespoon olive oil

200g lean minced beef

375g jar spaghetti sauce

1 packaged pizza base
(about 27cm across)

$1/4$ cup tomato paste

$1/2$ cup grated cheese

★ *Serves 2 to 4*

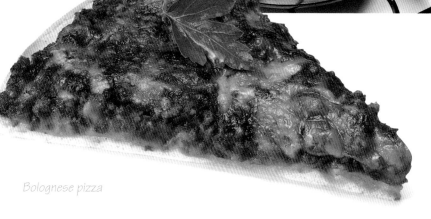

Bolognese pizza

1 Turn the oven to 230°C. Slice the mushrooms on a chopping board. Put a medium frying pan on the stove, turn the heat to high, and put the oil in the pan. Wait 30 seconds then add the mushrooms. **Stir the mushrooms with a wooden spoon until they are soft.**

2 Add the minced beef to the pan, and **stir with a wooden spoon until the beef is browned all over.**

3 **Add the spaghetti sauce to the pan** and stir with a wooden spoon to mix together. Simmer without a lid for 5-minutes or until the sauce thickens slightly.

4 Put the pizza base on a pizza tray or large oven tray. Spread the tomato paste over the top of the pizza base with a spoon. **Spread the beef mixture over the pizza base** and sprinkle with the cheese. Put the pizza in the oven and bake for 15 minutes or until the cheese is melted and the edge is crisp.

Cabanossi and capsicum pizza

Just cheese pizza

1 packaged pizza base
  (about 27cm across)

1/4 cup tomato paste

1/2 cup grated mozzarella cheese

1/2 cup grated cheddar cheese

1/2 cup grated parmesan cheese

★ *Serves 2 to 4*

ingredients

Cabanossi and capsicum pizza

2 sticks cabanossi

1 medium red capsicum

1 packaged pizza base
  (about 27cm across)

1/4 cup tomato paste

2/3 cup grated cheese

★ *Serves 2 to 4*

1 Turn the oven to 230°C. Put the pizza base on a pizza tray or large oven tray. Spread the tomato paste over the top of the pizza base with a spoon. Mix the three cheeses together **then sprinkle them over the pizza.** Put the pizza in the oven and bake for 8-minutes or until the cheese is melted and the edge is crisp.

1 Turn the oven to 230°C. On a chopping board, cut the cabanossi into thin slices. Wash the chopping board. **Cut the capsicum in half, remove the seeds and cut it into strips.**

2 Put the pizza base on a pizza tray or large oven tray. Spread the tomato paste over the top of the pizza base with a spoon. Sprinkle half the cheese over the pizza. **Sprinkle the cabanossi and capsicum over the pizza base** then the rest of the cheese. Put the pizza in the oven and bake for 15 minutes or until the cheese is melted and the edge is crisp.

Just cheese pizza

4 medium potatoes

2 tablespoons olive oil

4 small fish fillets

2 tablespoons plain flour

1 egg

$1/2$ cup cornflake crumbs

cooking-oil spray

★   *Serves 4*

fish'n'chips

You need to start this dish about 1-hour before you're ready to eat. We used boneless shark fillets, but any thick white fish fillet (that is, one with no bones) will work.

Fish 'n' chips

1 Before you turn on the oven, put 1 shelf in the lowest position and 1 shelf in the middle of the oven. Turn the oven to 230°C. Peel the potatoes on a chopping board then, **using a crinkle cutter, cut them into 1.5cm chips.** Put the chips and the oil into a large baking dish and stir to mix together. Put the chips on the middle shelf in the oven and bake, uncovered, for 20-minutes. Rinse the chopping board. On the chopping board, cut the fish into strips about 4cm wide.

2 Put the flour, egg and cornflake crumbs in 3 separate shallow bowls. **Toss 1 piece of fish in the flour then shake off the extra flour.**

3 Using a fork, beat the egg until it all becomes the 1 colour. **Dip the fish in the egg** then let the extra egg run off. Toss the fish in the cornflake crumbs. Dip the rest of the fish pieces in the flour, egg and crumbs, 1 piece at a time.

4 Lightly spray an oven tray with cooking-oil spray. **Put the fish on the tray and spray the fish with some more cooking-oil spray.**

5 Using oven mitts, take the chips out of the oven and place the dish on a wooden board. **Using an egg slice, and being careful not to burn yourself, turn the chips.** Put the chips back on the middle shelf of the oven for 30-minutes or until they are browned. When the chips have 10 minutes left to cook, put the fish on the lower shelf of the oven as well. Cook fish, uncovered, for 10 minutes or until it is cooked through. To see if the fish is cooked, gently break 1 piece open with a fork to see if it is a solid white colour inside.

Serve the fish with the chips.

excellent
roast dinner

A chicken that weighs 1.5kg is sometimes labelled as a size 15. You need to start making this roast dinner about 2 hours before you're ready to eat. See the instructions on the following pages.

Excellent roast dinner

1 medium onion

1 tablespoon butter

1½ cups fresh white breadcrumbs

1 egg yolk

½ teaspoon dried mixed herbs

1.5kg chicken

1 medium onion, peeled, extra

¼ cup olive oil

4 medium potatoes

1 tablespoon plain flour

1½ cups water

1 teaspoon chicken stock powder

★ *Serves 6*

1 Before you turn on the oven, put 1 shelf in the lowest position and 1 shelf in the middle of the oven. Turn the oven to 200°C. Finely chop the onion on a chopping board then wash the board. Put a medium frying pan on the stove and turn the heat to medium. Put the butter and onion in the pan and stir until the onion is soft. Let the onion mixture cool for 5 minutes. Put the breadcrumbs in a medium bowl then **add the onion mixture, egg yolk and mixed herbs.** Stir to mix together.

2 Rinse the chicken inside and out under cold water, then pat it dry with kitchen paper. Put the chicken on a chopping board, **use your hands to push the breadcrumb mixture into the chicken.** Wash the chopping board.

3 Tuck the tips of the wings under the chicken then **tie the chicken legs together with kitchen string.**

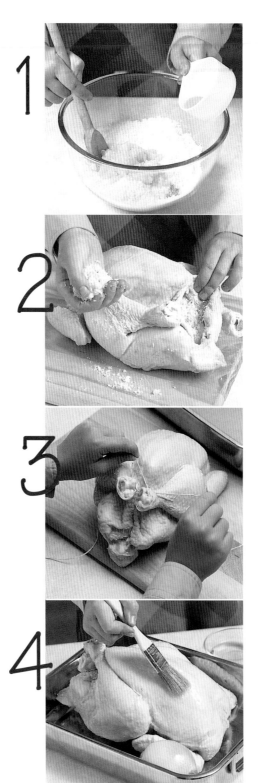

4 Put the chicken and the whole extra onion in a flameproof baking dish. Tuck the flap from the neck under the chicken. **Brush the chicken with 1 tablespoon of the oil.**

5 Peel the potatoes, wash them and pat them dry with kitchen paper. Cut the potatoes in half on a chopping board. **Put the potatoes into another baking dish and brush with the rest of the oil.** Put the potatoes on the lower shelf of the oven and the chicken on the shelf that is in the middle of the oven then bake for 30 minutes. Using oven mitts, take the potatoes out of the oven and put the dish on a wooden board. Leave the chicken in the oven. Close the oven door then turn the oven down to 180°C. Turn the potatoes over with tongs and put them back into the oven for another 45 minutes.

6 Using oven mitts, carefully take the chicken out of the oven and put the dish on a wooden board. Move the potatoes to the shelf the chicken was on in the oven and bake for another 10 minutes. **Using a skewer, pierce the chicken between the leg and thigh and look at the juices that run out.** If the juices are clear the chicken is cooked, if they are pink, put the chicken back into the oven until they are clear when tested with the skewer. Using tongs, put the chicken and onion onto a large plate and cover with foil to keep warm.

7 While the potatoes finish cooking, make the gravy by putting the baking dish which had the chicken in it on top of the stove and turn the heat to medium. **Add the flour and whisk until the mixture is bubbling.**

8 Using oven mitts, take the baking dish from the stove and put it on a wooden board. Mix the water and stock powder together in a small jug and **gradually whisk the stock mixture into the flour mixture.** Using oven mitts, put the dish back on the heat and whisk the gravy until it boils and thickens slightly. Place a large jug in the sink then put a strainer on top. Being careful not to burn yourself, pour the gravy through the strainer into the jug. Remove the potatoes from the oven and serve with the chicken, onion and gravy. Don't forget the seasoning (the breadcrumb mixture inside the chicken) which is delicious.

The ice-cream should be made a day before you're ready to eat. Make the fudge sauce just before you're ready to serve the sundaes.

1 Put the cream, condensed milk and vanilla essence into the large bowl of an electric mixer. Turn the mixer onto low, then medium, **then beat on high speed for about 5 minutes or until the ice-cream mixture is very thick.**

hot chocolate
fudge
sundaes

ingredients

600ml thickened cream

400g can sweetened condensed milk

2 teaspoons vanilla essence

hundreds and thousands

Chocolate fudge sauce

150g dark chocolate

1/2 cup thickened cream

10 white marshmallows

★ Serves 6

2 **Spoon the ice-cream mixture into a 15cm x 25cm loaf pan.** Cover it with aluminium foil and put it in the freezer for at least 3 hours or until it is frozen.

3 **Chocolate fudge sauce** Put a medium saucepan on the stove. Break up the chocolate and put it into the pan with the cream and marshmallows. Turn the heat to low **then stir until smooth.** This sauce must not get too hot and must never boil. Pour the sauce into a heatproof jug. See page 86 for instructions on melting chocolate in the microwave oven.

4 **Using an ice-cream scoop, put some ice-cream into each of 6 serving glasses.**

To serve, drizzle the hot chocolate fudge sauce over the ice-cream and sprinkle with the hundreds and thousands.

The condensed milk and the cream need to be refrigerated for at least 1 hour before you start to make the ice-cream.

Hot chocolate fudge sundaes

ingredients

cooking-oil spray

2 egg whites

1½ cups icing sugar mixture

⅓ cup boiling water

300ml cream

250g strawberries

1 kiwi fruit

2 passionfruit

★ *Serves 6*

Because the pavlova needs time to bake and cool, you have to start making it about 3 hours before you're ready to eat, or you can make the pavlova shell the day before and store it in an airtight container.

anna's
pavlova

1 Turn the oven to 180°C. Spray an oven tray with cooking-oil spray. Cover the tray with a sheet of baking paper. **Use a round cake pan or a plate that measures 20cm across to draw a circle on the paper.**

2 Put the egg whites in the small bowl of an electric mixer. **Sift the icing sugar through a strainer into the same bowl.**

3 Add the water then beat on high speed for 7 minutes. **Turn the mixer off.**

4 **Using a metal spoon, drop big spoonfuls of the meringue into the centre of the circle on the prepared oven tray.** Put the pavlova in the oven and bake it for 10 minutes. Turn the oven down to 150°C then bake for another 45 minutes. Turn the oven off, and leave the pavlova to cool in the oven with the door open a little bit. (Put the handle of a wooden spoon between the door and the oven— this will keep the door ajar and stop it being accidentally closed.)

5 When the pavlova shell is cool, **use the base from a flan tin (like the one used for quiches) to help move it to the serving plate.** You do this by putting the base of the flan tin between the paper and the shell then pushing the shell gently onto the plate.

6 Pour the cream into the small wbowl of an electric mixer and beat on medium speed until the cream is thick. Use a spatula to scrape the cream from the bowl onto the pavlova and to spread it out gently. Cut the tops off the strawberries then cut the strawberries into quarters on a chopping board. Peel the kiwi fruit then cut it in half and slice each half thickly. Cut the passionfruit in half and scoop the pulp into a small bowl. **Decorate the pavlova with the strawberries, kiwi fruit and passionfruit pulp.**

You can tint the meringue for the pavlova different colours for different occasions, like green for Saint Patrick's Day. Just add a couple of drops of food colouring to the meringue about 1 minute before the end of the beating time.

Anna's pavlova

This pudding is magic—you pour water over the top and it turns into chocolate sauce at the bottom! It takes quite a while to cook, so start making it about 1 1/4 hours before you're ready to eat.

chocolate pudding

60g butter

1/2 cup milk

1 cup self-raising flour

1 tablespoon cocoa powder

3/4 cup caster sugar

1 teaspoon vanilla essence

cooking-oil spray

3/4 cup firmly packed brown sugar

1 tablespoon cocoa powder, extra

2 cups boiling water

2 teaspoons icing sugar mixture

★ Serves 6

1 Turn the oven to 180°C. Put a large saucepan on the stove and turn the heat to medium. Add the butter and milk, and **stir until the butter is melted.**

2 Move the pan from the stove to a wooden board. Sift the flour and cocoa through a strainer into a medium bowl. Stir the caster sugar and vanilla essence into the warm butter and milk. **Stir in the cocoa mixture until mixed together.**

3 Lightly spray a deep ovenproof dish (it should be big enough to hold 6 cups of liquid) with cooking-oil spray. **Pour the chocolate mixture into the dish.**

4 **Use a spoon to push the brown sugar and the extra cocoa through a strainer** evenly over the chocolate mixture.

5 **Gradually pour the boiling water over the back of a wooden spoon onto the chocolate mixture.** Put the pudding in the oven and bake it for 50 minutes. Using oven mitts, take the pudding out of the oven and put it on a wooden board. Push a skewer into the centre of the pudding to see if it is cooked. If the skewer comes out clean, the pudding is cooked. If the mixture sticks to the skewer when it comes out, put the pudding back in the oven for about 5 minutes or until it is cooked when tested again. Leave the pudding for 5 minutes then sift the icing sugar over the top to serve.

Chocolate pudding

You need to start these about 5 hours before you want to eat them as the jelly needs time to set. We have used strawberry jelly but any flavour would be great, so choose your favourite!

ingredients

1/3 cup custard powder

2 tablespoons caster sugar

2 1/2 cups milk

2 cups boiling water

85g packet strawberry
  jelly crystals

8 strawberries, for decorating

★ *Serves 4*

1 Put the custard powder and sugar in a small jug then stir in 1/2 cup of the milk. **Keep stirring until all the lumps have gone.**

2 Put a small saucepan on the stove. Pour the rest of the milk into the pan, turn the heat to medium and heat the milk until bubbles form at the edge. Do not let the milk boil. **Give the custard powder mixture a good stir then quickly stir it into the milk.**

3 **Stir the custard until it boils and becomes thicker.** Pour the custard into a heatproof jug.

jelly
custard
cups

4 While the custard is cooling a little, pour the boiling water into a large heatproof jug. **Sprinkle the jelly crystals into the jug,** and stir until the crystals are dissolved and the mixture is clear.

5 Put 4 serving glasses on a tray (they should be big enough to hold about 1 cup of liquid each). Pour the jelly evenly into the glasses. Stir the custard **then pour it slowly over the jelly.** Move the jug from side to side to make patterns in the jelly. Leave the glasses on the tray, cover each with plastic wrap and put the tray in the refrigerator for about 4 hours or until the jelly is set.

Just before serving, decorate the tops with the strawberries.

Jelly custard cups

fruit chunks with honey yogurt

ingredients

200g tub vanilla yogurt

small pinch of cinnamon

1 tablespoon honey

1 banana

1 tablespoon lemon juice

2 kiwi fruit

250g strawberries

★ Serves 4

Fruit chunks with honey yogurt

1 **Put the yogurt, cinnamon and honey in a bowl** and mix together with a spoon.

2 Peel the banana and slice it on a chopping board. **Toss the banana in a small bowl with the lemon juice** (the juice will stop the banana from turning brown).

3 Peel the kiwi fruit and cut them into thick slices. Wash the strawberries. **Put them on a chopping board and cut them in half.** Serve the fruit with the yogurt dip.

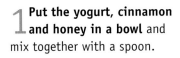

It's best to cut up the fruit just before you want to eat, but the yogurt dipping sauce can be made a day before. Just store it, covered with plastic wrap, in the refrigerator. Change the fruit to suit your taste and the season.

ingredients

¹/₂ cup thickened cream

1 teaspoon icing sugar mixture

¹/₂ cup Nutella

¹/₂ cup chopped mixed nuts

¹/₂ cup hundreds and thousands

¹/₂ x 300g packet mini grissini
   (Italian bread sticks)

★ *Makes 2 cups*

Crunchy choc-topped
bread sticks

1 Pour the cream into the small bowl of an electric mixer, add the icing sugar then beat on medium speed until the cream is thick. **Turn the mixer off.**

2 **Stir the Nutella into the cream mixture until it is mixed through.**

To serve, put the nuts, the hundreds and thousands and the Nutella mixture in 3 separate serving bowls. Dip the mini grissini into the Nutella mixture, then roll them in the nuts or the hundreds and thousands for a crunchy topping.

crunchy
choc-topped
bread sticks

Make the heart (Steps 1 and 2) the day before you are going to eat it so the ice-cream has time to freeze again.

ingredients

4-litre tub neapolitan ice-cream
600ml thickened cream
1/4 cup icing sugar mixture
few drops pink food colouring
small lollies, for decoration

★ *Serves 8*

marbled
ice-cream
heart

1 Take the ice-cream out of the freezer. Leave it for about 10 minutes or until it is just soft enough to remove from the container. **Using a large metal spoon, fill a 25cm heart-shaped cake pan (it should be big enough to hold 11 cups of liquid) with all the ice-cream.**

2 Cover the top of the ice-cream with plastic wrap. **Press down on the plastic until the ice-cream just squashes into the pan and the top is flat.** Leave the plastic wrap on the ice-cream and put the pan in the freezer until the ice-cream is frozen (this will take about 8 hours).

3 Using a tea towel (the pan will be very cold), take the ice-cream out of the freezer. Remove the plastic wrap then run a knife around the inside edge of the pan. Put about 3cm of warm water in the sink and hold the pan in the water while you count slowly to 5. This will melt the ice-cream a little and help the pan come off easily. Then **putting a tea towel over the pan to catch the drips, turn it upside-down onto a serving plate.** Lift off the pan, cover the ice-cream loosely with plastic wrap and return it to the freezer for 30 minutes.

4 Pour the cream into the small bowl of an electric mixer. Add the icing sugar and turn the mixer onto low then medium speed until the cream thickens. Turn the electric mixer off. Put a quarter of the cream aside in a small bowl until you are ready to decorate the top. **Add a few drops of pink food colouring to the rest of the cream and stir to mix together.**

5 Take the ice-cream heart out of the freezer and remove the plastic wrap. **Quickly spread the top and side of the heart with the pink cream.** Put a large star tube into a large piping bag and spoon in the uncoloured cream. Decorate the top with the plain cream and sprinkle the lollies over the top. (If the ice-cream begins to melt at any time while you are decorating the heart, put it back in the freezer to set.) Return the heart to the freezer until you are ready to serve.

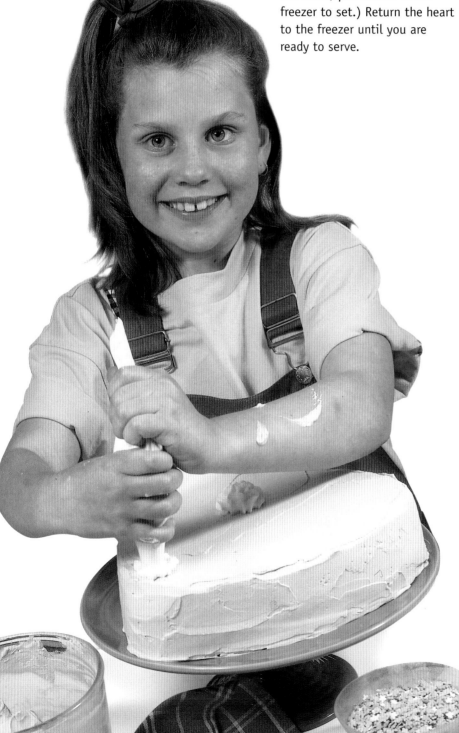

Marbled ice-cream heart

bread and butter
pudding

ingredients

8 slices white bread

30g butter

$1/4$ cup apricot jam

$2^{1/2}$ cups milk

3 eggs

2 tablespoons caster sugar

1 teaspoon vanilla essence

$1/2$ cup sultanas

$1/4$ teaspoon ground nutmeg

★ *Serves 4 to 6*

Bread and butter pudding

This pudding takes about 1 hour to cook, so start making it about 1¹/₂ hours before you're going to eat. If you don't like apricot jam, try using strawberry or plum jam.

1 Turn the oven to 160°C. Put the bread on a chopping board and spread 1 side of each slice with the butter then the jam. Cut the crusts off the bread and **cut each slice into 4 triangles.**

2 Put a medium saucepan on the stove. Pour in the milk, turn the heat to high and heat the milk until bubbles appear at the edge, then take the pan from the stove and put it on a wooden board. Break the eggs into a large jug. Add the sugar and vanilla to the eggs, and whisk until mixed together. Carefully pour in half the hot milk and whisk until mixed together **then pour in the other half and whisk again until mixed together.**

3 Put half the bread triangles, jam-side up, in a shallow ovenproof dish (it should be big enough to hold 5 cups of liquid) so they are slightly overlapping. **Sprinkle with half the sultanas.** Make a second layer with the rest of the bread triangles and the sultanas.

4 **Slowly pour the milk mixture over the bread triangles** then sprinkle over the nutmeg.

5 Put the ovenproof dish into a baking dish. **Using a jug, pour hot water (from the tap, not boiling from the kettle) into the baking dish to come halfway up the sides of the ovenproof dish.** Very carefully put the baking dish into the oven and bake the pudding for 1 hour or until it is just firm.

chocolate
mousse

Chocolate mousse takes about 2 hours to set, so you need to start making it at least 3 hours before you plan to eat.

Melting chocolate in the microwave oven

A quick and easy way to melt chocolate is in the microwave oven. Break the chocolate into pieces and put them into a medium microwave-safe bowl. Put the bowl in the microwave oven and cook on HIGH (100%) for 1 minute. Using oven mitts, take the bowl out of the microwave oven and stir the chocolate. Repeat the cooking and stirring 2 more times for another 30 seconds each time or until the chocolate is just melted.

Chocolate mousse

ingredients

200g dark chocolate

600ml thickened cream

3 eggs

$^1/_3$ cup caster sugar

50g dark chocolate, extra

8 sponge finger biscuits

★ *Serves 8*

1 **Break the chocolate into pieces and put it into a small heatproof bowl** which will sit over a small saucepan without slipping. Put this pan on the stove. Using a kettle, pour in enough boiling water to half fill the pan then turn the heat to high. Bring the water to the boil then turn the heat to low so the water is simmering.

2 Carefully put the bowl of chocolate over the pan of simmering water. When the chocolate starts to melt, stir it gently until it is completely melted. **Using oven mitts or a pot holder, carefully take the bowl from the pan and pour melted chocolate into a large bowl.**

3 Put half the cream into the small bowl of an electric mixer and beat it on medium speed until it thickens. **Turn the electric mixer off.**

4 Break the eggs into another small bowl of an electric mixer, add the sugar then beat on high speed for 3 minutes or until the mixture is very pale and thick. **Turn the electric mixer off.**

5 **Use a large wire whisk to gently stir the cream into the melted chocolate** then gently stir in half the egg mixture until the chocolate and egg mixtures are mixed together. Do the same thing with the rest of the egg mixture. Put 8 serving bowls on a tray (they should be big enough to hold about $^3/_4$ cup of liquid each). Spoon the mousse into the bowls and cover each with plastic wrap. Put the tray in the refrigerator until the chocolate mousse is just firm and well chilled.

6 **Using a vegetable peeler, peel the side of the extra chocolate into a small bowl.** This will give you tiny curls of chocolate. Whip the other 300ml of cream then put a spoonful on top of each mousse. Sprinkle the chocolate curls over the top and put the biscuits in the side of the whipped cream.

Make the pops and iceblocks a day ahead so that they have time to set.

ingredients

Mango pops

450g can mango slices

1/3 cup caster sugar

1 cup water

300ml thickened cream

★ *Makes 8*

1 Put a strainer in the sink and pour in the mango slices, letting the syrup drain away. **Put the mango slices in a bowl and using a spoon put them in a blender.** Blend the mango slices until they are smooth.

2 Put a medium saucepan on the stove. Put the sugar and water in the pan and turn the heat to medium, then stir until the sugar is dissolved and the mixture is clear. Stop stirring and simmer, without a lid, for 8 minutes. Carefully pour the sugar mixture into a heatproof jug—it should measure 1/2 cup. If you have too much liquid, cook it for a bit longer. If you have too little, add enough water to the jug to make 1/2 cup. **Pour the sugar mixture into the mango puree in the blender and blend until mixed together.**

3 Pour the cream into a medium jug, then **stir in 1/2 cup of the mango mixture.** Pour the rest of the mango mixture out of the blender into another medium jug.

chill out

4 Put 2 x 4-iceblock moulds (they should be big enough to hold 1/2 cup of liquid each) on a tray. Pour the cream mixture into the iceblock moulds and freeze them for 1 1/2 hours or until the pops start to set. **Take the pops out of the freezer and push an iceblock stick into each, then pour the rest of the mango puree into the moulds.** Return the pops to the freezer overnight so they are frozen solid.

Mango pops

1 **On a chopping board, cut the rind from the watermelon.** Cut the pink flesh of the watermelon into pieces.

2 **Put the watermelon into a food processor and process only until it turns to juice and the seeds are still whole.** Put a medium saucepan on the stove. Put the sugar and water into the pan and turn the heat to medium, then stir until the sugar is dissolved and the mixture is clear. Stop stirring and simmer, without a lid, for 8 minutes. Carefully pour the sugar mixture into a heatproof jug—it should measure 1/2 cup. If you have too much liquid, cook it for a bit longer. If you have too little, add enough water to the jug to make 1/2 cup.

3 Pour the watermelon juice through a strainer into a large jug and throw away the seeds. You need 2 cups of the juice. **Pour the sugar mixture into the juice** and stir to mix together. Put 2 x 4-iceblock moulds (they should hold about 1/2 cup liquid each) on a tray. Pour the watermelon mixture into the moulds, then put them in the freezer for about 1 1/2 hours or until the iceblocks start to set.

ingredients

Watermelon iceblocks

1kg piece watermelon

1/3 cup caster sugar

1 cup water

★ *Makes 8*

Watermelon iceblocks

4 **Take the iceblocks out of the freezer and push an iceblock stick into each** then put the iceblocks back in the freezer and leave them overnight so they will be frozen solid.

Try making them with rockmelon or honeydew melon as well.

It's best to make the cakes a day ahead so that they have time to cool before you decorate them.

ingredients

370g packet rich chocolate
  cake mix

60g soft butter

2 eggs

1/3 cup water

1/2 cup sour cream

1/4 cup Nutella

30g Flake bar

1 cup milk chocolate Melts

300ml thickened cream

1 tablespoon icing sugar mixture

250g fresh strawberries

★ *Serves 6 to 8*

1 Before you turn the oven on, move a shelf to the middle of the oven and put the 2 empty 20cm round sandwich cake pans on the same shelf to make sure they fit without touching. Take the pans out and turn the oven to 180°C. Grease the pans and cover the bases with baking paper (see page 11). Empty the contents of the packet cake into the large bowl of an electric mixer. Add the butter, eggs, water, sour cream and Nutella. Beat on low speed until everything is mixed together. Turn the electric mixer to medium speed and beat for 1 more minute. Turn off the mixer. Use a spatula to scrape down the sides of the bowl. **Crumble the Flake with your fingers and add it to the cake mixture.** Beat the mixture on medium speed for 1 minute then turn the mixer off.

2 Using a spatula, scrape the mixture off the beaters into the bowl then **divide the cake mixture between the 2 prepared pans.** Smooth the top of each cake mixture with the spatula.

3 Put the 2 pans on the middle shelf of the oven and bake them for 25 minutes. Using oven mitts, take the pans from the oven, place them on wire cake racks and test the cakes with a skewer (see page 10). Leave the cakes in their pans on the cake racks for 5 minutes. **Turn the cakes over onto the racks** and remove the pans then the baking paper. Place another cake rack over 1 of the cakes then, holding the 2 racks firmly like a sandwich, turn over so the cake is the right way up. Repeat with the second cake and let both cakes sit on their racks until they are cold.

4 While the cakes are cooling, grease an oven tray then cover the base with a piece of baking paper about 20cm x 25cm. Put the chocolate Melts in a medium heatproof bowl which will sit over a medium saucepan without slipping. Put this pan on the stove and, using a kettle, pour in enough boiling water to come 4cm up the side of the pan. Turn the heat to high. Bring the water to the boil then turn the heat to low so that the water is simmering. **Carefully place the bowl of chocolate over the pan of simmering water. When the chocolate begins to melt, stir it gently.**

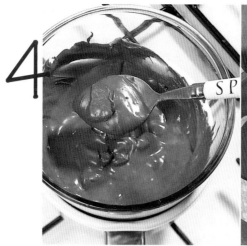

awesome chocolate cake

5 When the chocolate is completely melted, use oven mitts to lift the bowl from the heat and **carefully spread the chocolate on the baking paper.** Leave the chocolate to set—it will take about 20 minutes. (You can also melt the chocolate in the microwave. See page 86 for how to do this.)

6 When the chocolate is set, turn it over, **peel away the baking paper** and break the chocolate into large pieces.

See over.

Awesome chocolate cake

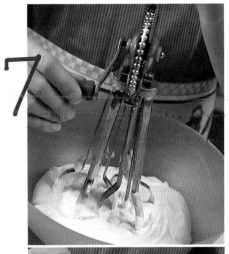

7 Put the cream and icing sugar in a small bowl and **beat with a rotary beater or with an electric mixer on medium speed until the cream is thick.** Cut the tops off the strawberries then cut the strawberries in quarters.

8 Place 1 cake into the centre of a large serving plate. Spread the top with half the cream **then place the other cake on top.** Spread the rest of the cream over the top of that cake.

9 Decorate the cake with the strawberries and chocolate pieces. It's best to do this about 1 hour before you're ready to eat. Put the cake in the refrigerator.

You can decorate these patty cakes just like we have, or you can use your favourite lollies to make up your own designs.

party patty cakes

ingredients

24 paper patty cases

125g butter

1 teaspoon vanilla essence

$3/4$ cup caster sugar

2 eggs

$1^1/2$ cups self-raising flour

$1/2$ cup milk

an assortment of lollies, licorice straps, chocolate sprinkles, desiccated coconut, food colourings for decorating

Vanilla butter frosting

30g butter

2 cups icing sugar mixture

2 tablespoons milk

1 teaspoon vanilla essence

food colouring of your choice

★ *Makes 24*

1 Check that a shelf is in the middle of the oven and that the 2 deep 12-hole patty pans fit (see page 90, Step 1). Turn the oven to 180°C. **Put the patty cases into the patty pans.**

2 Put the butter, vanilla essence and sugar in the small bowl of an electric mixer, then **beat on high speed until the mixture is pale and creamy.**

3 Break 1 egg into a small jug and **add it to the butter mixture.** Beat on high speed until the egg is mixed in. Do the same thing with the other egg.

4 Put the butter mixture in a large bowl then sift half the flour through a strainer into the bowl. Add half the milk and **stir until both the flour and the milk are mixed in.** Then do the same thing with the rest of the flour and milk.

5 **Using a tablespoon, put the cake mixture into the patty cases in the pans.**

6 Put the pans in the oven and bake for about 15 minutes or until the cakes are lightly browned. Using oven mitts, take the pans out of the oven and put them on a wire cake rack to cool for 15 minutes. **When they are cold, take the cakes out of the pans.**

7 **Vanilla butter frosting**
Put the butter in a medium bowl then sift half the icing sugar through a strainer over it. Add half the milk and all the vanilla essence, then **stir until the mixture is smooth.** Do the same thing with the rest of the icing sugar and the milk. Divide the icing among some small bowls and colour each with a few drops of the food colouring of your choice.

To make coloured coconut put some desiccated coconut into a small plastic bag then add a few drops of the food colouring of your choice. Seal the bag then shake it and rub the bag in your hands until the coconut is coloured. Spread the vanilla butter frosting over the tops of the cakes then decorate with the lollies, licorice, chocolate sprinkles and coloured coconut, using our designs as your guides.

Anzac slice

ingredients

1 cup rolled oats

1 cup plain flour

1 cup firmly packed brown sugar

$1/2$ cup desiccated coconut

125g butter

2 tablespoons golden syrup

1 tablespoon water

$1/2$ teaspoon bicarbonate of soda

★ *Makes 30*

This slice is a great lunch box treat. It will keep in an airtight container for about 4 days so you can make it on the weekend to take to school.

Anzac slice with sultanas

Anzac slice

1 Turn the oven to 160°C. Grease a 26cm x 32cm Swiss roll pan and cover the base with baking paper (see page 11). Put the oats, flour, sugar and coconut in a large bowl and **stir to mix together.**

2 Chop the butter. Put a medium saucepan on the stove and turn the heat to medium. Put the butter, golden syrup and water in the pan and **stir the mixture with a wooden spoon until the butter is melted.**

3 Take the pan off the stove and put it on a wooden board. **Add the bicarbonate of soda to the butter mixture** (it will froth and bubble).

4 **Pour this butter mixture into the oat mixture** and stir with a wooden spoon until all the ingredients are mixed together.

5 Sprinkle the mixture evenly into the prepared pan, **then press down on the slice with your hands until it is flat.** Put the pan in the oven and bake the slice for 35 minutes (it should feel firm when you touch it). Using oven mitts, take the pan out of the oven and place it on a wooden board. Leave the slice in the pan to cool for about 15-minutes. Turn the slice over onto the wooden board and remove the pan then the baking paper. Cut the slice into pieces about 5cm square.

You can make the slice different if you want to—try adding 3/4 cup dark chocolate Bits, or 3/4 cup sultanas, or 3/4 cup chopped dried apricots in with the oats (see Step 1).

Anzac slice with dried apricots

Anzac slice with dark chocolate

orange juicy cake

This is a great quick-mix cake for all occasions. You can serve this cake warm for dessert with cream or ice-cream, or you can eat it cold as a snack.

ingredients

125g soft butter

1/3 cup milk

2 eggs

1 tablespoon finely grated
   orange rind

2 tablespoons orange juice

1 cup caster sugar

1 1/2 cups self-raising flour

1 tablespoon icing
   sugar mixture

1/2 cup orange juice, extra

2 teaspoons icing sugar
   mixture, extra

1 medium orange

★   Serves 6 to 8

Orange juicy cake

1 Before you turn the oven on, move a shelf to the middle of the oven. Turn the oven to 180°C. Grease a deep 20cm round cake pan then cover the base with baking paper (see page 11). **Put the butter, milk, eggs, rind, juice, sugar and flour in the large bowl of an electric mixer.** Beat ingredients on low speed until mixed together.

2 Turn the speed to medium and beat for about another 3 minutes or **until the cake mixture is lighter in colour and smooth.**

3 **Pour the cake mixture into the prepared pan, using a spatula to scrape out all the mixture.** Put the pan in the oven and bake the cake for 45 minutes. Using oven mitts, take the pan out of the oven, place it on a wire cake rack, and test the cake with a skewer (see page 10). Leave the

pan on the wire cake rack to cool for 5-minutes. Turn the cake over onto the wire cake rack, remove the pan and peel the baking paper away from the cake. Place another cake rack over the cake then, holding the 2-racks firmly like a sandwich, turn over, so the cake is the right way up (see page 11).

4 Put a tray under the wire cake rack. **Sift the icing sugar through a strainer over the hot cake.**

5 **Slowly pour the extra orange juice over the cake.** Sift the extra icing sugar through a strainer over the juice. Slice the orange on a cutting board then cut each slice in half. Use orange slices to decorate the cake.

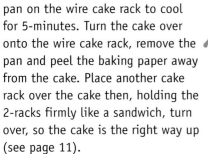

These all-time favourites can be frozen for up to a month after you have made them. They don't take long to defrost, so make lots of them to keep in the freezer for emergencies!

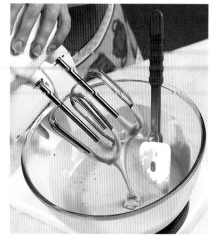

ingredients

2 eggs

1¹/₃ cups firmly packed brown sugar

1 cup plain flour

³/₄ cup self-raising flour

¹/₂ teaspoon bicarbonate of soda

¹/₂ cup vegetable oil

1 cup chopped unsalted
  roasted peanuts

1 cup dark chocolate Melts, halved

¹/₂ cup white Choc Bits

★ *Makes 24*

1 Before you turn the oven on, move 2 oven shelves so that they are both as close to the middle of the oven as possible. Turn the oven to 200°C. Grease 2 oven trays. Put the eggs and sugar in the large bowl of an electric mixer then beat on high speed for about 1 minute or until the mixture is pale brown. **Turn off the electric mixer and scrape the sides of the bowl with a spatula.**

2 **Sift both the flours and the bicarbonate of soda through a strainer over the egg mixture.**

3 Add the oil, peanuts, dark chocolate Melts and Choc Bits to the bowl and **stir to mix together.**

4 Scoop out some of the cookie mixture with a tablespoon, **roll it into a ball with your hands,** and place on prepared trays. Repeat rolling, place balls 6cm apart.

mega choc-chip cookies

5 Continue making balls of cookie mixture and placing them on the trays. **Flatten the balls with your hand to make a 5cm round shape.** Put the trays in the oven and bake the cookies for 10 minutes or until lightly browned. Using oven mitts, take the trays out of the oven, place them on a wooden board, and leave them for 5 minutes. Using an egg slide, lift the cookies onto a wire cake rack to cool. Repeat Steps 4 and 5 with the rest of the cookie mixture.

Mega choc-chip cookies

You need overripe, almost black, bananas for this recipe because they give the best flavour. If your bananas are not ripe enough, put them in a paper bag in a cool place (not the refrigerator) for a day or 2.

bananarama

ingredients

4 medium overripe bananas

125g soft butter

1 teaspoon vanilla essence

1/2 cup caster sugar

2 eggs

1 tablespoon milk

1 1/2 cups self-raising flour

1 teaspoon bicarbonate of soda

1/2 teaspoon ground cinnamon

Cream cheese frosting

1 1/2 cups icing sugar mixture

125g packaged cream cheese

30g soft butter

1 teaspoon grated lemon rind

★ Serves 6

1 Before you turn the oven on, move a shelf to the middle of the oven. Turn the oven to 180°C. Grease a deep 20cm round cake pan, then line the base with baking paper (see page 11). **Put the bananas into the large bowl of an electric mixer and mash them with a fork until almost smooth.**

2 Add the butter, vanilla essence, sugar, eggs and milk to the bowl. Sift the flour and bicarbonate of soda through a strainer into the bowl. **Beat the cake mixture on medium speed for 4 minutes or until it is pale in colour.**

3 **Pour the cake mixture into the prepared pan, using a spatula to scrape out all the mixture.** Put the pan in the oven and bake the cake for 1-hour. Using oven mitts, take the pan out of the oven, place it on a wire cake rack and test the cake with a skewer (see page 10). Leave the pan on the cake rack to cool for 5 minutes. Then turn the cake over onto the rack, remove the pan then peel the baking paper away from the cake. Place another cake rack over the cake then holding the 2 racks firmly like a sandwich, turn over, so the cake is the right way up. Leave the cake to cool completely.

4 **Cream cheese frosting** Sift the icing sugar through a strainer into the small bowl of an electric mixer. Chop the cream cheese. Add the cream cheese, the butter and the rind to the icing sugar. **Beat the mixture on medium speed until the frosting is smooth.**

5 **Spread the frosting over the top of the cake** and sprinkle it with the cinnamon.

ingredients

175g butter

3/4 cup caster sugar

3/4 cup firmly packed
   brown sugar

3 eggs

1/2 cup plain flour

1/3 cup self-raising flour

1/3 cup cocoa powder

2 teaspoons drinking chocolate

2 teaspoons icing sugar mixture

★ Makes 24

bonza brownies

You can keep these brownies in an airtight
container for up to 3 days ... if they last that long!

1 Before you turn the oven on, move a shelf to the middle of the oven. Turn the oven to 180°C. Grease a 19cm x 29cm slice pan and line the base and sides with baking paper (see page 11). The paper must come 3cm above all 4 edges of the pan. Chop the butter and put it in a small saucepan on the stove and turn the heat to medium. Put the caster sugar and brown sugar in a large bowl. **When the butter is melted, pour it into the bowl and mix together with a whisk.**

2 Break 1 egg into a jug then **pour it into the bowl with the sugar and whisk to mix together.** Repeat this step with the rest of the eggs.

3 Sift both the flours and cocoa through a large strainer into the sugar mixture, **then whisk to mix together.**

4 **Pour the brownie mixture into the prepared pan, using a spatula to scrape out all the mixture.** Put the pan in the oven and bake for 15 minutes. Put a sheet of foil over the top of the brownie and continue baking for another 45 minutes. Using oven mitts, take the pan out of the oven and stand it on a wire

cake rack. Put a skewer into the centre of the brownie to see if it is cooked. If the mixture sticks to the skewer when it comes out, put the brownie back in the oven for another 5-minutes and test it again. Leave the brownie in the pan on the wire cake rack until it is cold.

5 **Using the baking paper, lift the brownie out of the pan and peel away the paper.** Cut the brownie into rectangles about 7cm x 9cm. Sift the drinking chocolate through a fine strainer over half the brownies and sift the icing sugar over the rest. (We used a plastic stencil to make the numbers.)

blueberry muffins

You can keep these muffins for a day after they are made in an airtight container, but they taste best when they are just cooked and still warm. It is best to use frozen blueberries straight from the freezer—don't let them thaw.

ingredients

2 cups self-raising flour

3/4 cup firmly packed brown sugar

1 egg

1 cup fresh or frozen blueberries

3/4 cup milk

1/2 cup vegetable oil

2 teaspoons icing
   sugar mixture

★ *Makes 6*

1 Before you turn the oven
  on, move a shelf to the
middle of the oven. Turn the
oven to 200°C. Lightly grease
a 6-hole Texas muffin pan (the
holes should be big enough
to hold about 3/4 cup of the
muffin mixture). **Put the flour
and sugar in a strainer and
use a wooden spoon to sift
them into a large bowl.**

2 Break the egg into a
  small jug and using a
fork, beat it until it becomes
1 colour. Add the beaten egg,
blueberries, milk and oil to the
flour mixture, **then stir until
just mixed together—do not
overmix.**

3 **Spoon the mixture
  evenly into the holes of
the prepared muffin pan.** Put
the pan in the oven and bake
the muffins for 25 minutes.
Using oven mitts, take the pan
out of the oven and put it on a
wire cake rack. Test the muffins
with a skewer (see page 10).

4 As soon as the muffins are
  cooked, **carefully tip them
out of the pan onto the wire
cake rack.** Just before you serve
the muffins, sift the icing sugar
over the top.

Choc-honeycomb muffins

You can make delicious
choc-honeycomb muffins by
changing the blueberry muffin
recipe. Just add 1/2 cup white
chocolate Bits and 100g chopped
chocolate-coated honeycomb
instead of the blueberries.

ingredients

125g butter

¾ cup condensed milk

½ cup firmly packed brown sugar

100g white chocolate

⅔ cup dried apricots

2 x 90g packets coconut macaroons

⅓ cup desiccated coconut

★ Makes 35

apricot chews

These chewy treats are perfect to snack on at school. They can be kept in the refrigerator, in an airtight container, for up to a week.

1 Grease a 19cm x 29cm rectangular slice pan, then line the base and sides with baking paper (see page 11). The paper must come 3cm above the edges of the pan. Chop the butter and put it in a medium saucepan on the stove. Stir in the condensed milk and brown sugar. Turn the heat to low and stir the mixture, without letting it boil, until the butter is melted and the sugar is dissolved. **Remove the pan from the heat and place it on a wooden board.**

2 Chop the chocolate and put it in the bowl of a food processor with the apricots and macaroons then process them until they are all finely chopped. **Tip the apricot mixture into the condensed milk mixture** and stir until they are mixed together.

3 **Spread the mixture into the prepared pan.** Cover the pan with plastic wrap and put it in the refrigerator for about 1 hour or until the mixture is firm.

4 Using the baking paper, lift the slice out of the pan, turn it onto a chopping board and remove the baking paper. Cut the slice into pieces about 4cm square. **Roll each square, with your hand, on a chopping board to make a log about 5cm long.**

5 **Roll the logs in the coconut and place them on a tray.** Put the tray in the refrigerator for about 1 hour or until the logs are firm again.

rocky road

Rocky road needs time to set so plan to make it at least 1 hour before you want to eat it. You can keep it in an airtight container in the refrigerator for up to 3 days. You will need 1 packet of marshmallows weighing 250g and 500g of Melts for this recipe.

ingredients

1 cup unsalted roasted peanuts

1/3 cup shredded coconut

3 1/3 cups milk chocolate Melts

4 cups small multicoloured marshmallows

★ Makes 24

1 Turn the oven to 200°C. Grease a 20cm x 30cm lamington pan then cover the base with baking paper (see page 11). Put the peanuts on an oven tray and the coconut on another oven tray. Put both trays in the oven and bake for 3 minutes. **Using oven mitts, take the tray with the coconut on it out of the oven and put it on a wooden board.**

2 Bake the peanuts for another 4 minutes or until they are lightly browned. **Using oven mitts, take the tray with the peanuts on it out of the oven and put it on a wooden board.**

3 Put the chocolate Melts in a medium heatproof bowl which will sit on top of a medium saucepan without slipping. Put this pan on the stove and, using a kettle, pour in enough boiling water to come 4cm up the side of the pan. Turn the heat to high. Bring the water to the boil then turn the heat to low so the water is simmering. Carefully put the bowl of chocolate over the pan of simmering water. **When the chocolate has started to melt, stir it gently.** When the chocolate is completely melted, use oven mitts to carefully remove the bowl from the heat and place it on a wooden board. (You can also melt the chocolate in the microwave. See page 86 for how to do this.)

4 Put the peanuts, coconut, marshmallows and melted chocolate in a large bowl and **stir until everything is coated in chocolate.**

5 Spoon the mixture into the prepared lamington pan and **spread it out with a spoon.** Cover the pan with plastic wrap and put it in the refrigerator for 30 minutes or until the chocolate is set.

6 **Tip the rocky road out on a chopping board.** Cut or break the rocky road into pieces about 5cm square.

¹/₂ cup flaked almonds

200g butter

¹/₃ cup honey

³/₄ cup instant malted milk powder

2 cups Rice Bubbles

2 cups Corn Flakes

1 cup plain cake crumbs

¹/₂ cup desiccated coconut

★ *Makes 20*

hubble bubble slice

1 Turn the oven to 200°C. Grease a 20cm x 30cm lamington pan, then cover the base and sides with baking paper (see page 11). The paper must come 3cm above the edge of the pan. Put the almonds on an oven tray and bake them for 5 minutes until lightly browned. Chop the butter and put it in a large saucepan on the stove. **Add the honey and malted milk powder.** Turn the heat to medium and stir the mixture until the butter is melted.

2 Take the pan from the stove and put it on a wooden board. **Add the rest of the ingredients** and stir to mix everything together.

3 Spoon the mixture into the prepared pan. **Using your hands, press the mixture down as firmly and as evenly as you can.** Cover the pan with plastic wrap and put it in the refrigerator for 1 hour until the slice is firm. Using the baking paper, lift the slice out of the pan onto a chopping board. Cut the slice into fingers.

This slice will keep for up to 3-days in an airtight container in the refrigerator. Use any plain cake (leftovers are good) to make the crumbs.

popcorn caramels

ingredients

12 large paper-lined
  foil patty cases

1/4 cup vegetable oil

1/3 cup popping corn

150g butter

250g packet
  Jersey Caramels

★ *Makes 12*

1 Put the patty cases into a 12-hole muffin pan (the holes should be big enough to hold about 1/3 cup of popcorn caramel mixture each). Put a large pan that has its own tight-fitting lid on the stove, put the oil in the pan and turn the heat to high. Wait 1-minute, then turn the heat to medium. **Add the corn to the pan** and immediately put on the lid. Using oven mitts, shake the pan a few times and leave the lid on until you can hear only a few popping noises. Remove the pan from the heat and tip the popcorn into a large bowl. You need 4 cups of this popcorn. (A few pieces of the corn won't have popped. Take these out and throw them away.)

2 Chop the butter and put it in the same large saucepan with the Jersey Caramels.

Put the pan on the stove and turn the heat to medium. **Stir until the caramels are melted and the butter and caramel is mixed together.** (The mixture will look quite oily at first, but after a while it will all mix together.)

3 Remove the pan from the stove and put it on a wooden board. Add the popcorn to the pan and **stir gently to mix everything together.**

4 **Spoon the popcorn mixture into the patty cases** and leave them for 10 minutes or until they are cold.

These crunchy treats will last for up to 2 days.

crunchy chocolate nut clusters

These are really yummy. If you can stand to give them away, they make a great gift—and your friends and relatives could see what a great cook you've become!

ingredients

1 cup milk chocolate Melts

50g chocolate-coated honeycomb bar

$^1/_3$ cup unsalted roasted peanuts

★ *Makes 15*

To Nanna
Love Jessica

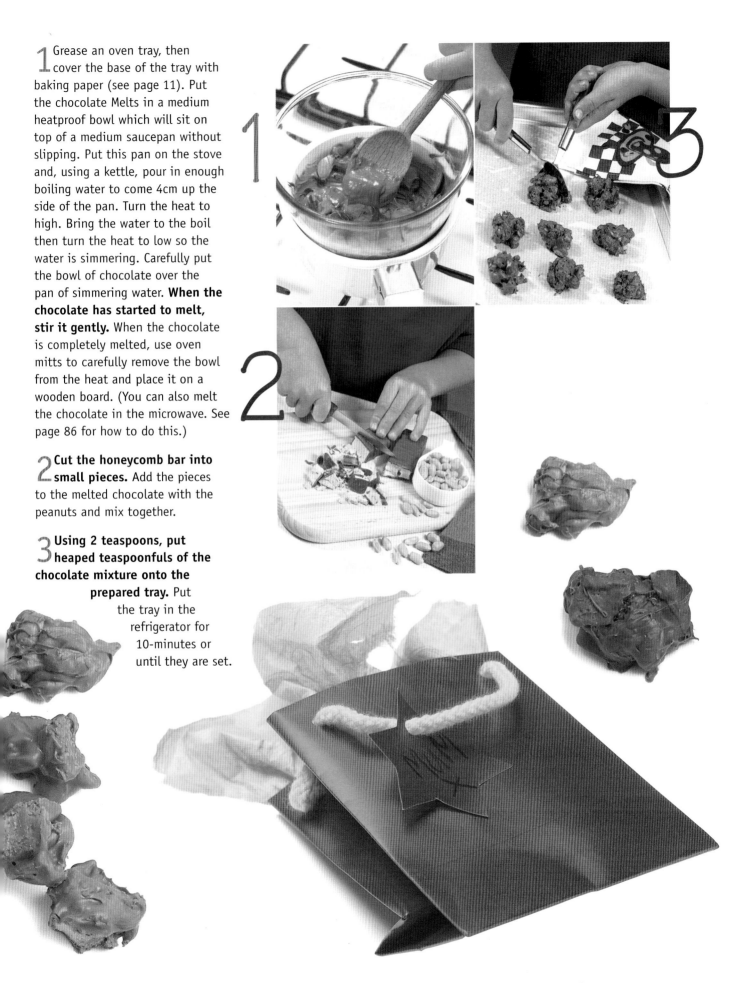

1 Grease an oven tray, then cover the base of the tray with baking paper (see page 11). Put the chocolate Melts in a medium heatproof bowl which will sit on top of a medium saucepan without slipping. Put this pan on the stove and, using a kettle, pour in enough boiling water to come 4cm up the side of the pan. Turn the heat to high. Bring the water to the boil then turn the heat to low so the water is simmering. Carefully put the bowl of chocolate over the pan of simmering water. **When the chocolate has started to melt, stir it gently.** When the chocolate is completely melted, use oven mitts to carefully remove the bowl from the heat and place it on a wooden board. (You can also melt the chocolate in the microwave. See page 86 for how to do this.)

2 **Cut the honeycomb bar into small pieces.** Add the pieces to the melted chocolate with the peanuts and mix together.

3 **Using 2 teaspoons, put heaped teaspoonfuls of the chocolate mixture onto the prepared tray.** Put the tray in the refrigerator for 10-minutes or until they are set.

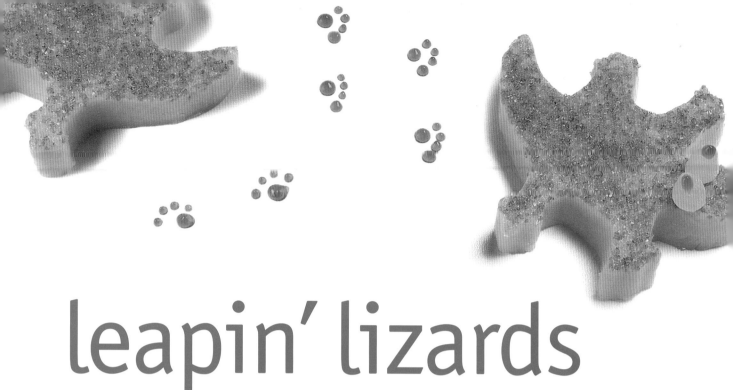

leapin' lizards

You can buy biscuit cutters in lots of shapes—from
stars to kittens to Christmas trees—but we used
one shaped just like a lizard for these white fudge
treats topped with fancy coloured sugar crystals.

ingredients

200g white marshmallows

60g butter

2 tablespoons water

2 x 200g blocks white chocolate

coloured sugar crystals

lollies, to decorate

1 **Place 2 strips of baking paper to cover the base** and sides of a deep 19cm square cake pan.

2 Place the marshmallows, butter and water in a small saucepan. Put the pan on the stove and turn the heat to low. **Stir until the marshmallows are melted.**

3 Meanwhile, break the chocolate into a small bowl. **Add the chocolate to the marshmallow mixture** and stir over low heat until it is melted (the mixture will become thick).

4 Pour the mixture into the prepared pan, **using a spatula to scrape out all the fudge.**

5 Sprinkle the top of the fudge with coloured sugar crystals. **Use your hand to pat down lightly.** Cover the pan with plastic wrap and place in the refrigerator for about 1 hour or until the mixture is set.

6 Use the baking paper to lift the fudge from the pan. **Using a decorative biscuit cutter, cut a shape from the fudge** starting at a corner. Decorate shapes with lollies if you like.

what food is that?

BACON RASHERS also called slices of bacon.

BICARBONATE OF SODA also called baking soda.

BUTTER use salted or unsalted ("sweet") butter; 125g is the same as stick of butter.

CHICKEN SEASONING a packaged mix of herbs and spices including sweet paprika, garlic, ginger and black pepper.

CHILLI SAUCE, SWEET a mild, Thai-style bottled sauce made from red chillies, sugar, garlic and vinegar.

Sweet chilli sauce

COCONUT
Desiccated dried and finely grated coconut.

Shredded thin strips of dried coconut.

CORN KERNELS also called niblets.

CREAM
Sour a thick, cultured soured cream.

Thickened a whipping cream which has a thickener.

EGGS some recipes in this book use raw or barely cooked eggs; be careful if there is a salmonella problem where you live.

ESSENCES also called extracts.

Vanilla essence

FLAKE a sweet bar made from thin layers of milk chocolate.

FLOUR
Plain also called all-purpose flour, made from wheat.

Self-raising plain wheat flour sifted with baking powder. You use 1 cup flour with 2-teaspoons baking powder to make self-raising flour.

FRENCH ONION SOUP MIX a packaged soup mix.

Jelly crystals

HUNDREDS AND THOUSANDS when you buy them, the container will have 100s & 1000s printed on the front.

JAM also called conserve.

JELLY CRYSTALS an instant mixture of powdered gelatine, granulated sugar, flavouring and colouring.

JERSEY CARAMELS sweets made from glucose, condensed milk, flour, oil and gelatine.

Jersey caramels

MUSTARD, DIJON mild French mustard.

MACAROONS, COCONUT meringue-like biscuits made from coconut, egg white and cornflour.

NOODLES, 2-MINUTE dried instant noodles, usually packaged with a sachet of flavour.

Coconut macaroons

2-minute noodles

NUTELLA chocolate-flavoured hazelnut spread.

Nutella

OIL
Cooking-oil spray vegetable oil in an aerosol can.
Sesame used a lot in Asian cooking, made from roasted and crushed white sesame seeds; it is used for flavouring, not for frying.

Vegetable a lot of different oils made from plants.

OYSTER SAUCE an Asian thick, rich, brown sauce made from oysters, salt and soy sauce.

PINEAPPLE THINS canned very thin slices of pineapple.

PITTA a round Middle-Eastern bread which can be split easily into 2 pieces to make a pocket.

PLUM SAUCE a thick, sweet and sour dipping sauce made from plums, vinegar, sugar, chillies and spices.

Pumpkin

PUMPKIN also called squash.

RANCH DRESSING a mild, tasty salad dressing made of buttermilk, oil, vinegar and spices.

ROLLED OATS also called oatmeal.

STOCK CUBES strong-flavoured small squares of dehydrated beef, chicken or vegetable stock; they can be very salty. Also called bouillon cubes.

SUGAR
Brown a soft, fine, granulated sugar with molasses which gives it its colour.

Stock cube

Caster also called superfine or finely granulated table sugar.

Icing sugar mixture also called confectioners' sugar or powdered sugar.

SULTANAS also called golden raisins or muscatels.

TACO SEASONING MIX a flavouring for Mexican food containing oregano, cumin chillies and other spices.

Sultanas

TOMATO SAUCE also called tomato ketchup or catsup.

Taco seasoning mix

index

ARE YOU MISSING SOME OF THE WORLD'S FAVOURITE COOKBOOKS?

The Australian Women's Weekly Cookbooks are available from bookshops, cookshops, supermarkets and other stores all over the world. You can also buy direct from the publisher, using the order form below.

TITLE	RRP	QTY	TITLE	RRP	QTY
100 Fast Fillets	£6.99		Indian Cooking Class	£6.99	
After Work Fast	£6.99		Japanese Cooking Class	£6.99	
Beginners Cooking Class	£6.99		Just For One	£6.99	
Beginners Thai	£6.99		Just For Two (Sep 07)	£6.99	
Best Food Desserts	£6.99		Kids' Birthday Cakes	£6.99	
Best Food Fast	£6.99		Kids Cooking	£6.99	
Breads & Muffins (Sep 07)	£6.99		Kids' Cooking Step-by-Step	£6.99	
Cafe Classics	£6.99		Low-carb, Low-fat	£6.99	
Cakes, Bakes & Desserts	£6.99		Low-fat Feasts	£6.99	
Cakes Biscuits & Slices	£6.99		Low-fat Food for Life	£6.99	
Cakes Cooking Class	£6.99		Low-fat Meals in Minutes	£6.99	
Caribbean Cooking	£6.99		Main Course Salads	£6.99	
Casseroles	£6.99		Mexican	£6.99	
Casseroles & Slow-Cooked Classics	£6.99		Middle Eastern Cooking Class	£6.99	
Cheap Eats	£6.99		Mince in Minutes (Sep 07)	£6.99	
Cheesecakes: baked and chilled	£6.99		Moroccan & the Foods of North Africa	£6.99	
Chicken	£6.99		Muffins, Scones & Breads	£6.99	
Chicken Meals in Minutes	£6.99		New Casseroles	£6.99	
Chinese & the foods of Thailand, Vietnam, Malaysia & Japan	£6.99		New Curries	£6.99	
			New Finger Food	£6.99	
Chinese Cooking Class	£6.99		New French Food	£6.99	
Christmas Cooking	£6.99		New Salads	£6.99	
Chocolate	£6.99		Party Food and Drink	£6.99	
Chocs & Treats (Oct 07)	£6.99		Pasta Meals in Minutes	£6.99	
Cocktails	£6.99		Potatoes	£6.99	
Cookies & Biscuits	£6.99		Rice & Risotto (Sep 07)	£6.99	
Cupcakes & Fairycakes	£6.99		Salads: Simple, Fast & Fresh	£6.99	
Detox	£6.99		Sauces Salsas & Dressings	£6.99	
Dinner Lamb	£6.99		Sensational Stir-Fries	£6.99	
Dinner Seafood	£6.99		Simple Healthy Meals (Sep 07)	£6.99	
Easy Curry	£6.99		Soup	£6.99	
Easy Midweek Meals	£6.99		Stir-fry	£6.99	
Easy Spanish-Style	£6.99		Superfoods for Exam Success	£6.99	
Essential Soup	£6.99		Sweet Old-Fashioned Favourites	£6.99	
Food for Fit and Healthy Kids	£6.99		Tapas Mezze Antipasto & other bites	£6.99	
Foods of the Mediterranean	£6.99		Thai Cooking Class	£6.99	
Foods That Fight Back	£6.99		Traditional Italian	£6.99	
Fresh Food Fast	£6.99		Vegetarian Meals in Minutes	£6.99	
Fresh Food for Babies & Toddlers	£6.99		Vegie Food	£6.99	
Good Food for Babies & Toddlers	£6.99		Wicked Sweet Indulgences	£6.99	
Greek Cooking Class	£6.99		Wok Meals in Minutes	£6.99	
Grills	£6.99				
Healthy Heart Cookbook	£6.99		TOTAL COST:	£	

Mr/Mrs/Ms _____

Address _____

_____ Postcode _____

Day time phone _____ email* (optional) _____

I enclose my cheque/money order for £ _____

or please charge £ _____

to my: ☐ Access ☐ Mastercard ☐ Visa ☐ Diners Club

Card number | | | | | | | | | | | | | | | | |

Expiry date _____ 3 digit security code *(found on reverse of card)* _____

Cardholder's name_____ Signature _____

To order: Mail or fax – photocopy or complete the order form above, and send your credit card details or cheque payable to: Australian Consolidated Press (UK), ACP Books, 10 Scirocco Close, Moulton Park Office Village, Northampton NN3 6AP.
phone (+44) (0)1604 642200
fax (+44) (0)1604 642300
email books@acpuk.com
or order online at www.acpuk.com
Non-UK residents: We accept the credit cards listed on the coupon, or cheques, drafts or International Money Orders payable in sterling and drawn on a UK bank. Credit card charges are at the exchange rate current at the time of payment.
Postage and packing UK: Add £1.00 per order plus £1.75 per book.
Postage and packing overseas: Add £2.00 per order plus £3.50 per book.
All pricing current at time of going to press and subject to change/availability.
Offer ends 31.12.2008

* By including your email address, you consent to receipt of any email regarding this magazine, and other emails which inform you of ACP's other publications, products, services and events, and to promote third party goods and services you may be interested in.